ADVENTURES
in MIXED MEDIA ART

Inspiration, Techniques
& PROJECTS FOR
Painting, Collage
& MORE

EDITED BY Amy Jones

NORTH LIGHT BOOKS
Cincinnati, OH
CreateMixedMedia.com

CONTENTS

MATERIAL CONCERNS?

Worried about all the materials you see on the
next page? Don't be! You can pick and choose
which ones you want to use, and you can reuse
many of the items in various projects.

MATERIALS LIST

24" × 34" (61cm × 87cm) acrylic sheet, 1/2" (13mm) thick

40" (102cm) 22-gauge wire

acrylic cutting knife

acrylic glazing liquid, satin (Golden)

acrylic paints in a variety of colors

Adobe Photoshop

airbrush paints

alcohol inks

aluminum sheets

assorted embossing templates

awl

brayer

bulldog clips

buttons or other embellishments

carbon paper

Chartpak Blender marker

cheese grater from dollar store, dental tools or any other hand-carving tools

Clayboards

collage elements including images and paper (collage paper, tissue paper, decorative paper)

copy paper

cotton rag

craft knife

crayons (optional)

cutting mat

decorative chipboard letters

fabric

felt

fluid acrylics

foam applicator or brush

foam mat or a piece of suede or leather

gel medium or collage medium

gesso

glitter

glue

glue stick

hair dryer

hammer

hard plastic case

ink-jet printer

instant coffee crystals

label maker (optional)

love notes

magazines

metal flakes

multi-textured yarn

nails

natural findings—twigs, strips of bark, approximately 1 1/2" × 7 1/2" (4cm × 19cm)

Neocolor II Crayons

oil pastels

old gift card for scraping

old hardcover book

paintbrushes appropriate for your chosen paints and mediums

palette

palette knife

palette paper

PanPastels

paper stumps

paper towels

Patina Green glaze (Golden)

pencil

soft pastels, a few monochromatic colors

pens of your choice

permanent black ink pad

photographs

piece of art

pieces from a wooden box, approximately 2 1/2" × 3" (7cm × 8cm)

plastic test tubes or vials

polymer or soft gel

pre-gessoed wood panel, canvas and canvas boards

quilter's wheel

razor blade

rubbing alcohol

sanding block

sandpaper

scissors

scrap corrugated cardboard

scrap paper

screening materials

screen-printing squeegee

setting mat

sewing machine and black thread

spiral-bound journal

spray bottle

Stabilo All pencil

stencils

straightedge

string from curtains

string or yarn

stylus

tape

Thermofax screen (optional)

thick, uncoated paper or cardstock

tracing paper or deli wrap

transparency paper

used tea bags, dried

vintage book pages and newspaper

vintage postage stamp

Walnut Stain Distress Ink (Ranger)

water

water container

watercolor paints

watercolor paper

wax paper

white gel pen

white pencil

white tissue paper

wire brush

wood glue

wooden button with one hole

wooden tag

INTRODUCTION

Welcome to your mixed-media adventure. If you're reading this right now, chances are you've been inspired by mixed-media art and are ready to give it a try. If you're worried about things like not being able to draw or being overwhelmed by all of the kinds of mixed-media techniques—don't be. Or maybe you haven't painted since your high school art class. Again, don't worry. This book will guide you through your voyage into mixed media with help from experts like Dina Wakley, Kelly Rae Roberts, Mary Beth Shaw and more.

In Chapter One, you'll take advantage of those inspired feelings with readings from *The Declaration of You!* and *Creative Thursday*. Not only will you be enthused to start making art, you'll find ideas for keeping that excitement alive throughout your journey.

With Chapter Two, you'll jump right in by making an art journal where you can experiment with the basic mixed-media techniques you'll need to make the art you want to make. Learn mark-making techniques from Jean Pederson. Create backgrounds and fun hand lettering from Carmen Torbus. Practice drawing and painting faces with Katie Kendrick, until you've overcome those initial worries.

Refine your mixed-media style in Chapter Three. You've mastered the basics, so now it's time to take it to the next level. Give one of your earlier art attempts a face-lift with "A New Weave" from *Mixed Media Revolution*. Try using unusual materials with techniques from Mary Beth Shaw and Serena Barton's *Wabi-Sabi Art Workshop*.

But this book is only the beginning so your adventure doesn't end there. Chapter Four shows you how to pass on your love of mixed media. Create hopeful messages for others to find, or work on a collaborative project with a friend. Show someone else how to start her mixed-media adventure.

Are you ready? Good. Now go create mixed media!

-Amy

1

MAKE THE MOST OF YOUR CREATIVE ENERGY

It's time to get excited. You're starting your artful journey right now by making the most of your creative energy. Jessica Swift and Michelle Ward lead the way by helping you discover and declare your enthusiasm. Then Marisa Anne has suggestions for finding inspiration in all aspects of your life and helps you find your own creative voice. With these readings, you'll be ready to start making mixed-media art. Fair warning: Be prepared to be inspired.

DECLARATION

ENTHUSIASM
from *The Declaration of You!*
by Jessica Swift and Michelle Ward

VISIT CREATEMIXEDMEDIA.COM/ADVENTURES-IN-MIXED-MEDIA FOR BONUS CONTENT.

ENTHUSIASM (DISCOVER IT)

You are allowed to like whatever you want, JUST BECAUSE, no reasons or excuses needed.

How's that for an opening? We believe in it so strongly that we have to bold it, open the book with it, and say it again: You are allowed to like whatever you want, JUST BECAUSE, no reasons or excuses needed.

Now, think about something you love that you wouldn't necessarily want to tell anyone about.

Real Housewives marathons.
Your Loch Ness Monster theories.
Your teen idolization of Kirk Cameron.
Your current idolization of Justin Bieber.

Sometimes we like things that we think we "shouldn't" like. (BAN "shouldn't" from your vocabulary from this moment forward!) But, the bottom line is that we like them, and there's absolutely nothing wrong with that. Not only is there nothing wrong with that, but it's what makes you you, and that's worth discovering, owning and shouting from the rooftops. (By the way, shouting doesn't have to mean literally shouting. We just want you to own it, and go confidently forth with it into the world!)

We're meant to be happy. Each and every one of us deserves it. Even if you think you don't deserve it and you have a laundry list of reasons why you don't, YOU DO.

When you're happy, you're putting your best self forward, sending inspired and passionate energy out into the world to affect all the other people who come into contact with you. We think our mission as humans is to be the best people we can be and to love each other, and we believe that can only occur when we're living the life that we're meant to live.

So if you're having a hard time embracing the idea that you can go down your own path (or give yourself the time and space to explore what you might love to do) for your own happiness, consider this: In embracing your own happiness, you're helping other people give themselves permission to be their own happiest selves. That's an important job, isn't it? And we each have it! We each have a unique formula to be our happiest and best selves, and shying away from it takes something away from not only you but from everyone in your world!

We think this happiness formula starts with defining our Big Likes. You can call your Big Likes whatever you want: passion, enthusiasm, interest, hobby . . . whatever word gets you into the mind-set. We realize everyone has her own association with words, which is why we encourage you to explore this. Basically, we want you to think about what makes you feel EXCITED. And "I don't know . . ." isn't an answer because everybody likes doing something. There are no wrong answers.

Maybe you really like to shop, but you're thinking, "My passion can't be shopping!" Or maybe you love to eat (note from Jess: Ahem, this is me), and you think, "But loving to eat? That's just being obsessed with food, not something I'm passionate about!" To which we say: Who the hell cares? Do you like it? Do you get excited about it? Great! Write it down on the worksheet that follows.

Confession from Jess—

Sometimes when I go to bed, I get really excited about getting to eat breakfast in the morning. You think I'm joking? Nope. It's true. I love to eat!

Write down the things you love and the things you love to do. If "love" is too strong a word, think of your "Big Likes." (Use the space on page 12 if you like.) If you're really, really, truly, honestly coming up with a blank, throw a notebook in your purse/pocket and carry it with you. Whenever you're having fun, looking forward to something, feeling happy/useful/ un-self-conscious/free/in touch, or seeing time go by at warp speed, write it down. It can be as simple as drinking a glass of wine in your backyard or as big as throwing your mom a surprise party with one hundred people. No holding back! Use the first column on the *Why I Like What I Like* worksheet and get it all down!

When you're done filling in column one, sit with the list and ask yourself, "What is it that I love about each of these things?" Jot these things down in the middle column. In the right column, write how each item makes you feel. Be as specific as possible.

Be selfish with the things that make you tick! Embrace them! Nurture them! We want you to be as happy as you can possibly be. (Happy people are the most fun to hang out with, just so you know.)

Jess says—

So, you now know I'm passionate about break-fast. I love breakfast dearly, and I eat it right when I wake up every morning. I make a smoothie pretty much every day, but not your ordinary, run-of-the-mill smoothie. My smoothies are concoctions made from things like bananas, spinach, parsley, soymilk, yogurt, flax oil, flax seeds, avocado, grapes and milk thistle. Are you grossed out? I know. My husband doesn't know how I drink it, but I'm telling you, it's delicious! (I think I have different taste buds than many people.) Anyway, I love starting my day this way. A smoothie followed by a cup of Earl Grey tea, and I'm ready to go. This is one of the pieces of my life that makes me tick. Some people (ummm, my husband) think it's weird, and I don't care because I love it. What do I love about it? Well, for one, it's pretty fun to blend things up in the kitchen and see what I can come up with! Plus, it offers me an oppor-tunity to treat my body nicely. How does it make me feel? I love it because it makes me feel healthy.

So you see? We're not necessarily talking about huge, lifelong, heart-on-fire passions here—though you can include those, too—but we're talking about all the little pieces of you that make up your life.

So, now that you've written down some things that you're excited about, maybe you're not feeling satis-fied with your list. Maybe you have an internal, "But I don't really know what I like to do" dialogue running through your head because you haven't allowed your-self the space to explore your interests for such a long time. That's OK! Take a few minutes to think about some things that pique your interest.

Have you recently been intrigued by yoga, but you haven't ever tried it? Maybe you think learning how to play an instrument could be kind of fun? What about just changing up your morning routine a little bit to see what changes in your life? Embrace the word "experiment," and make note of at least five things that you wanna try. Scratch that—we're not even going to go that far yet. Make a note, instead, of at least five things that you might wanna try. Use the *Things I Might Want to Try* worksheet (on page 13) to jot down your might-wanna-try ideas.

TOPIC: Why I Like What I Like

Things I love/big like	What do I love about it?	How does it make me feel?

thedeclarationofyou.com

Want to know the method behind our madness? The reason we asked you for the "why" is that it's probably not the actual task that enthuses you, but the reason behind it. Going back to Jess's smoothie example, the actual smoothie isn't really what she loves—it's knowing that she's starting her day in a healthy, delicious way, and that's what revs her engine. Do you see any threads between the reasons behind the things you *might* wanna try and why you love the things that you *know* you love? What drives you to do something that you want to do and/or try something new? What are the components? The emotions? The results? Sum 'em up by finishing the following sentence:

I like what I like because what I like causes me to feel _____.

Which leads us to your declaration! Using the statement you wrote above, declare below how your socks get rocked!

ENTHUSIASM DECLARATION

I declare that doing things that make me feel _____
_____
_____ **makes me tick!**

I like what I like just Because:

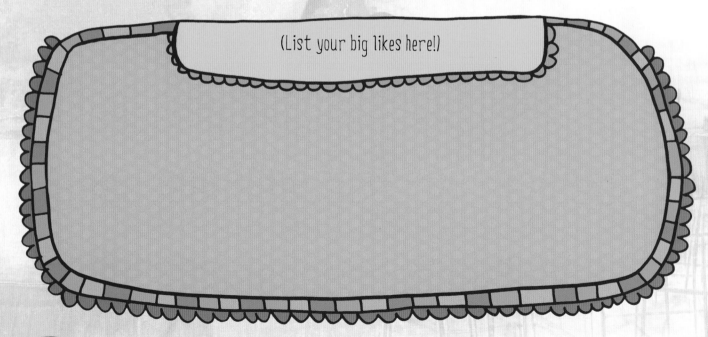

(List your big likes here!)

TOPIC: Things I Might Want to Try

I might want to try...	because...

thedeclarationofyou.com

GOING IN SEARCH OF INSPIRATION

Because it is all too easy to get caught up in our day-to-day lives, many of us find ourselves in a place where we feel more numb than engaged. We may not yet be in the habit of cultivating moments for inspiration. Much like taking time for creativity is undervalued, so is taking time for stillness.

So how do you start? You start with taking time for stillness and then you start with what you love. This applies to anything and everything that brings you the most joy. What are you doing when you lose all sense of time? It can be watching a movie, listening to music, enjoying a wonderful meal, sipping the best glass of wine, reading a good book, listening to a radio program or podcast, surfing your favorite blogs, flipping through a magazine, going to a museum or taking a walk. If you don't have a clue where to start, thinking of it this way can help: If you had all the time and money in the world, what would you do first? And if a nap is the first thing that comes to mind, do it! A nap is an excellent choice and probably means that you need some rest. Never underestimate the power of a nap to begin tapping into your inspiration. I often get entire painting ideas that appear right between my sleep and wake state.

GOING IN SEARCH OF INSPIRATION
from *Creative Thursday* by Marisa Anne

Being well rested is key and the best state to be in when beginning your search for inspiration. Self-care plays a critical role in a happy life. I think many of us are depleted of rest as well as lacking quality nourishment and exercise. All of those things we're so busy trying to do? We can't do any of them without a healthy body—from which also comes a healthy mind. When a person's health is compromised, nothing else works. We are reminded of this when suddenly we get a cold or the flu and are stopped cold in our tracks. I like to consider creativity as a key element of that ritual of self-care, equally as important as rest, nourishment and exercise. But creativity does not happen to its fullest potential unless the other three are being attended to. Simply put, are you drinking enough water throughout your day? That's all I'm asking. And if you need a nap before you start thinking about any of the topics I've shared with you so far, please put this book down and get some rest.

Taking time for rest, stillness and creativity is not indulgent, it is a must.

BE ON THE LOOKOUT FOR SPONTANEOUS INSPIRATION.

It's magical—that moment when inspiration floats in and you feel so energized that it's all you can do to keep from acting on your new idea right away. I like to call this "spontaneous inspiration," and it usually happens when you are in the flow of your life. You know, those days when you are having so much fun and everything just seems to be going your way? Many times you might be out of your usual routine; you might have the day off, or you might be traveling. I find that traveling is a perfect way for me to bump into spontaneous inspiration. Anything that takes me out of my usual routine makes me more attuned to my surroundings. When you are experiencing this kind of living, everything can become a source of inspiration.

It's important to develop an acute awareness and receptivity to inspiration, and not become muted by

certain kinds of daily routine. And I say "certain kinds" because some routines—taking a walk in nature or sitting outside in your garden, enjoying quiet time each morning through meditation or while sipping a cup of coffee or tea—support and encourage your continued connection with spontaneous inspiration.

FIND TIME FOR YOGA AND EXCERCISE.

Exercise does not always carry with it the best connotation for fun, so we don't always equate it to being another tool for finding inspiration, but it is clearly an aspect of self-care, therefore we cannot dismiss its contribution to our creativity. As much as I like my naps, I have also had some of the best painting ideas during yoga class—and not just during the restorative poses.

There are many different types of yoga and after trying several, I settled into the practice of Iyengar yoga. This precision-based yoga uses an intense mental focus on the physical aspects of each pose, to not only strengthen the body, but to calm the mind. Finding more ways to cultivate a happy mind allows your creativity to thrive.

So you would think it would be easy for me to incorporate more yoga into my life, right? Yes, but it takes time and practice to incorporate new ways of being into our daily lives. It takes commitment combined with patience—honoring the step-at-a-time that we do take.

Maybe you, too, have found a form of exercise that inspires you, or maybe you haven't noticed the inspiration yet, because your tired muscles are screaming at you. But have you noticed the change in your mental state? You are on your way to being inspired. A lot of times we seek an activity that relaxes or even distracts our mind just enough to make room for some inspiration to sneak in. Exercise supports this effort.

TRY A CHANGE OF SCENERY.

Change your location. Sometimes that's all you need to do to mix things up a little. And that can even mean moving around in your own home. Working from home, I find this necessary. That is why if you don't find me on the floor, you will find me with my laptop located in different parts of the house at various times throughout the day. I don't know what it is about sitting on the floor or the ground, but it seems to make me feel more in touch with my inspiration. Come to think of it, it is probably because sitting on the floor is slightly out of the ordinary from my usual routine of sitting at my desk or in a chair or on the sofa. Having a laptop certainly allows me to mix up my seating and those subtle changes in my workspace as well.

Sometimes I even pick up my paints and move them to different rooms or outside.

Although routine is good—especially for keeping us grounded—it can also leave inspiration a little stale. Every time you break your routine just a little, the new shift in perspective can inspire many new ideas. For me, this is especially true when I actually leave my home.

I love my home and I love working from home, which means I also love staying home—sometimes for days at a time. This choice is intentional for a couple of reasons. One is that I work best on a project when I have uninterrupted focus, enough to gain some momentum, which I use to carry me through the completion of the project. I also like to refer to this as a "mode." For instance, if I am in creative mode, I like to stay in that mode as long as I can without switching to bookkeeper mode or packing-and-shipping-orders mode or running-errands mode. The other reason is that living in Los Angeles and relying upon a car to get around, maneuvering through traffic, struggling to find parking can take a lot of energy out of a person.

The downside to sequestering oneself at home for extended periods is that it can result in what we often refer to as "cabin fever." You might love being at home so much that you honestly don't even recognize cabin fever is happening. Suddenly your focus becomes less sharp, and it can feel like you're frittering away time. This is right about the time when crankiness begins to set in. And the desire to stay home and get yet one more thing done will completely override the need for a break. That's the exact time to remember: Breaks and naps are good for you! They are vital. A break from work, a break from routine, a break from location can be just the thing to give you a new perspective.

DRAW OR WRITE IN A SKETCHBOOK OR JOURNAL.

Author Julia Cameron is known for encouraging artists to practice a daily habit of "morning pages" to keep the flow of creativity going, and I would encourage that same practice with a sketchbook. I think we often feel that we must have an idea to start drawing, but many times sitting down with my sketchbook and allowing the pencil to move freely across the page is exactly where my new idea is born. The key words here are "move freely." In order to summon ideas this way, the usual suspects—judgment or self-criticism— must be kept at bay. Rather than feeling intimidated (again) by that blank page, in a sketchbook or journal, it must become an invitation to play—a place to meet up with new inspiration.

I've found that drawing regularly keeps a steady flow of ideas coming. New characters almost always appear first in the pages of my sketchbook. This is when I have to be especially careful to hold back judgment of anything that shows up on the pages of a sketchbook. In fact, sometimes I won't even recognize that I like a character right away. Because it's brand-new, it might take some time before it grows on me. I realize this when I flip back through the book sometime later and say, "Hey, look at that little fellow. I'd like to incorporate him into this painting." Other times I do have an idea of a new character, and I work him out through loose renderings before I paint.

If you don't know where to start in a sketchbook, just start moving your pencil or pen around the page, just like you would start a doodle. It might start with one line or the repeating of one shape over and over. If I'm feeling at a loss about where to start when that pencil hits the paper, I start with a circle. I might even go over it and over it again until I feel ready to move the pencil in a new direction.

It can be challenging to create without judgment or expectation in the way we did when we were kids, but when doing initial concepting, it's one of the most important times to foster a safe and supportive environment. Sketchbook work or journaling is a delicate time when inspiration is being fed, and new ideas are being born.

LEARN SOMETHING NEW.

I remember how excited I was to finally be out of school. And, because I had been so excited to be out of a classroom setting, it took me quite a while before I felt ready to be a student again. Yet being a student is one of the best ways to spark inspiration. It wasn't until I started teaching that I realized just how much I had missed being a student.

For artists looking to expand their creative toolbox, it's essential to find the right kind of class. By "right kind of class" I mean one that is led by a teacher who creates a safe environment that encourages your creative self versus a teacher who wants to criticize. I have had several moments in my artistic life where I have been shut down, and had I taken those moments to heart, I would have stopped creating forever.

As I mentioned before, art and creativity are completely subjective, and while technique and certain kinds of aesthetic can be taught, a good teacher will know how to teach these skills while also supporting pure creativity.

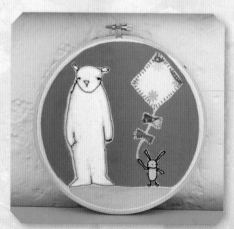

VISIT CREATEMIXEDMEDIA.COM/ADVENTURES-IN-MIXED-MEDIA FOR BONUS CONTENT.

While creative classes are perfect for furthering your skill set, they are not the only kind of class that will spark inspiration. In fact, I think taking a class in something entirely new stretches you past your comfort zone, giving you that shift in perspective again. One of two things can happen when you take a class; you might come out of it not liking what you learned, or you might love it so much that it is life-changing in the most powerful way. Both possibilities will teach you more about who you are—what you do or don't like. Gaining that understanding about yourself is essential to finding your true creative voice.

Thanks to the Internet, there are now countless opportunities to learn from people all over the world who can inspire and/or challenge you. There's almost no excuse not to venture out and take a new class. You don't even have to leave the comfort of your home to learn. Exposing yourself to something entirely new will not only increase your skill level and build your knowledge base, but it might open you up to a possibility that you had no idea you would love so much.

EXPLORE OTHER EXAMPLES OF CREATIVITY.

Certainly a trip to a museum to see an exhibition is on the agenda as an artist. Traffic and limited parking aside, one of the benefits of living in or visiting a city such as Los Angeles is that it offers so many kinds of exhibitions. There's nothing more inspiring than experiencing great art up close and in person.

I know that living in a visually saturated world, artists can also be hesitant to see too much work from others for fear that it may overinfluence their own expression. But no matter how much art is being created and shared—especially online—seeing what others create can be enriching. Our job as artists is to see what we like in the world and to be able to translate it and express it in such a way that it becomes uniquely ours. This is especially true of those of us who work professionally. While mimicry of artists who inspire us is often how we start out creating, moving away from that is exactly how we learn to develop our own style.

Use the influence of work you admire as a jumping-off point to your own expression. While you don't want this influence to supercede your own creative ideas, you also don't want to stop appreciating others' work simply because we are too fearful of all looking the same. One of my early mentors said, "There are no new ideas. What makes something new is our take on it."

KEEP IN A CONSTANT FLOW.

The beauty of inspiration is that once you know how to summon it, it will always come again. Even on the days when it feels like inspiration might have gone missing, it is never far. Now that I'm practiced at being in the flow of new ideas, it is becoming my way of living, and it's almost like I can't shut it off—not that I want to. But now I get so many ideas that I can hardly keep up with them all. That is why keeping a pen and paper and/or your smartphone nearby is perfect for catching inspiration, so you can return to it when you are ready.

Appreciate where you are and what you already have. There is no better way to stay in the flow than a state of gratitude, and there's nothing that shuts down inspired ideas more than intense dissatisfaction with where you are. Since we never get it all done, we are always on our way somewhere. While looking forward to what's ahead is exciting, there is also always so much to appreciate right where we are. A daily gratitude list works wonders for getting you happy right now.

FINDING YOUR VOICE

It's right about now, with all of this encouragement to increase self-awareness, that I'm realizing this book is bordering on becoming more than just a book on creativity, because here's the thing: The practice of creativity and knowing who you are go together. You just can't express one without the other. The best and quickest way to find your creative voice is to practice daily creating. The more you create, the closer you will get to discovering or even stumbling into your unique point of view. It can't help but reveal itself to you through your process. This approach is also known as "working quick and fast to get you out of your head," so that self-judgment barely has a chance to make an appearance.

KNOW YOURSELF.

If you are uncertain about who you really are, the practice of daily creating will not only help you find your creative style, but it will help you find your voice. And if you already think you know who you are, you will only come to know yourself better.

When you start creating like this—creating regularly and producing a lot of work—you begin to recognize all the areas of your life where you have been living a little bit of a lie. Because we are so conditioned to please others from the time we are little, we rarely stop and ask ourselves if what we are living is what we truly want and genuinely reflects who we are. We are not encouraged to express our individuality as much as we are encouraged to fit in. Oh, maybe a little individuality is encouraged, but it can't be too individual because it still has to conform to certain standards to be acceptable either to our parents, our schools, or later, at our place of work. It becomes an individual's responsibility to know (and continually discover) who she truly is.

So how do you get to know yourself? First you decide to be totally honest with yourself about your life. Then you spend time with you. You look out into the world, and you form preferences about what you

like and what you don't like, from beliefs to clothing styles to ways of being in the world to design to food, music, movies, places to live, places to travel to . . . you name it, you can have a feeling about it one way or another. And this is the part you want to pay the closest attention to, your initial response to anything put before you.

VISIT CREATEMIXEDMEDIA.COM/ADVENTURES-IN-MIXED-MEDIA FOR BONUS CONTENT.

Often we have an initial feeling about something, but we sway it, or morph it to fit in with whatever group we currently want to be accepted into. This is not to say that being genuinely open to others' opinions and ideas isn't a nice trait to have. It is. We are all different, and being open to our differences can inspire and challenge our thoughts (and art) further. However, just be sure to acknowledge your first response to anything, which doesn't mean that your first response is always accurate, but it will give you more clues about who you are. This is also referred to as listening to your intuition, your heart, your gut.

Those who have become great leaders and creative visionaries have often been the first to follow a belief that very few, if any, had. They were willing to pave the way for us because they knew who they were and were not willing to compromise their beliefs so someone else would understand or like them better or even support them on their journey. They just believed and went for it.

Chances are, if you are ready to open up more to your creative self, or you are already accessing your creativity, you are a visionary. Artists transform the world. Sometimes I wonder what the world would be like if we were all tapping into our inner artist.

FINDING YOUR VOICE
from *Creative Thursday* by Marisa Anne

So are you spending enough quality time with you? Are you listening to your intuition? If you want to get to know someone else, you spend time with them, and you listen closely to what they are sharing about themselves and their ideas, right? This is what you want to do with you. If your life is full and surrounded by others with very little time for yourself—especially time alone—it may mean that you have been avoiding getting to know yourself.

This can be scary for those of us who have spent years fitting in, doing the "right" thing for everyone everywhere and saying yes to everything that is asked of us. No matter where you are on your journey, you have to be willing to ask yourself some questions to reacquaint yourself with you. These may be questions you have been avoiding for a long time, but your creative voice lies within the answers. If you want to express who you truly are, you must know who you truly are.

While the questions I've included for you here seem simple, thinking about them can unearth a lot. Sometimes your answers might not fit with your current lifestyle, which might mean that your life is ready for some big changes. So, it is important for me to note that you are in control here, and you don't have to make any changes that you are not ready for. Asking the questions and contemplating the answers only means that you will be thinking about something new; it doesn't mean you have to take action immediately.

Asking and answering questions throughout your life invites expansion, clarity and . . . change. If that is unsettling, it's understandable. But, ideally, we all want to grow to the place where this feels exciting for us, where we welcome each and every opportunity to evolve and change because that is what is life-giving and what inspires our creativity.

As much as there are days when I wish that I could just figure it all out once and for all, I now know that continually searching for and finding the answers is what feeds me. Life is an ever-evolving journey that we take. So let's have more fun with it all, and let's use it to endlessly feed ourselves and our art. I was watching an interview with famed American portrait photographer Annie Leibovitz, who after almost forty years of continuously exploring photography still comes across new ways to pursue her art. She said that every time she tries something new, she realizes "just how deep that well really is."

2

DISCOVER YOUR SIGNATURE STYLE

You've found your inspiration and now it's time to jump right in and learn those basic mixed-media techniques. First, you'll make a journal. Don't worry; it's easier than it sounds, I promise. Then you'll use this "Book of Dreams" journal to respond to the writing prompts provided by Sheri Gaynor and try the art journaling exercises from the Journal Fodder Junkies. You can practice making background layers, discover your own signature hand-lettering styles and experiment with painting in your journal, too. When you're feeling secure in what you've learned, be brave and move out of your art journal and onto canvas boards. Put together all the techniques you learned to create your first works of art.

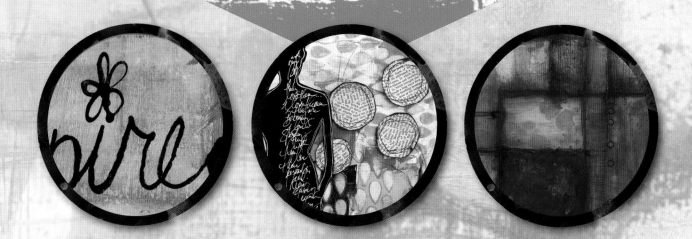

THE BOOK OF DREAMS JOURNAL

Having rounded up your gear and started preparations for your journey, your first task is to create your Book of Dreams Journal. You will use this journal with "Charting the Course" (see page 31).

Your journal will hold all your intentions, dreams and field notes to help you create a vision for your life. It will become a visual and written guidebook, a place you can visit over time and return to, especially if you feel you have lost your way.

A few words about my own journals. My Book of Dreams Journals are rough-and-tumble—kind of like me—all muss and no fuss. I want them to be a place where I can work intuitively. I spill my intentions and dreams to the page without worrying about perfection or the end result. I don't always want to know where I am going. I want to see what unfolds, what is beneath the layers—basking in pleasant surprise. On my pages, you'll see bubbles, blobs, tears and spills—the rough edges that make up my dreams.

Using your intuition is a big piece of reaching for your dreams. Dreams are not tidy; they can be random, and sometimes wild, so I invite you to let go and trust. Take risks, make a mess. In the end it really doesn't matter. What you want is to unlock the door, to have the Universe dance and play with you. If you get caught up in the details, the outcome or how it looks, you might miss out on a truly extraordinary discovery.

MATERIALS LIST

5" × 5" (13cm × 13cm) sheet of aluminum (TENseconds Studio)

acrylic glazing liquid, satin (Golden)

acrylic paint-Phthalo Green, Blue Shade

alcohol inks

assorted embossing templates

craft knife

foam applicator

foam mat or a piece of suede or leather

gel medium

gesso

glitter

palette

paper stumps

paper towels

paste paper or decorative paper

Patina Green glaze (Golden)

quilter's wheel

scrap paper

spiral-bound journal

stylus

tape

wax paper

white pencil

wire brush

THE BOOK OF DREAMS JOURNAL
from *Creative Awakenings* by Sheri Gaynor

VISIT CREATEMIXEDMEDIA.COM/ADVENTURES-IN-MIXED-MEDIA FOR BONUS CONTENT.

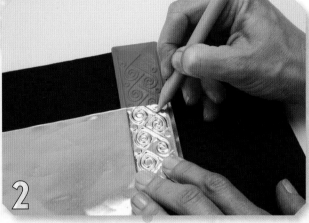

On a scrap of paper, create some sort of symbolic drawing of your own (it can be very simple) and center it over the back of the aluminum sheet. Working on the foam mat (or a piece of suede) and using a pointed stylus, trace the image. (Remember, what you are tracing on the back will be reversed on the front side.) Set the aluminum on the first embossing template you wish to use and burnish it with a paper stump tool, as if you were doing a charcoal rubbing.

After you can see the general pattern, emboss the detail a bit further with a smaller stump.

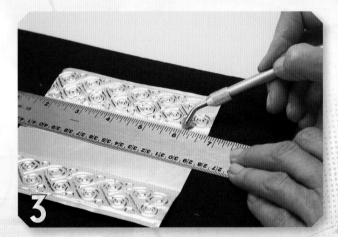

Repeat the pattern on the other side of the sheet. Use a quilter's wheel to create a dashed line inside both halves of the patterned area.

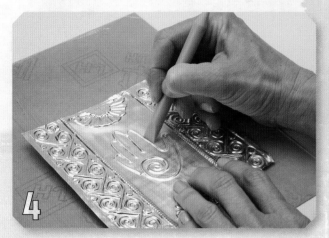

4 Use a small wire brush to give some texture to the center portion. Continue embossing from both sides, as you see fit, using a stylus to sharpen details when necessary.

5 You are now ready to add color to the metal. Squirt some of the alcohol ink onto a palette and then pick it up with a felt applicator and rub the color on. Start with one color and rub it on. (Use a paper towel to blot excess ink and smooth out uneven areas.)

6 Continue building up layers of color until you have the look you like. Apply gel medium to an area of the metal where you would like to have some glitter, and sprinkle some over the wet medium.

7 Tap off the excess glitter and apply a second color of glitter if you like. When the gel medium is dry, scrape away any glitter that may be on areas where you don't want it. Apply additional medium over the glitter to seal it.

8 When the piece is dry, position it on the front of your journal where you would like it to be visible through a window (which you'll create in the next step). Trace around it using a white pencil.

9 With the cover open and placed on a cutting mat, use a craft knife and a metal ruler to cut along the lines. Be mindful not to overcut the corners. Open the journal to expose both the front and back covers and put wax paper under each. Cover the boards with gesso. Crumple up a paper towel and create texture over the gesso to disguise the brushstrokes.

10 To get between the spaces of the coil, lift the board up to the coil as much as possible and brush right over the wire and onto the board. Don't worry if you get gesso on the coil; you can wipe it off when it's wet or scrape it off when it's dry.

11 Let the gesso dry. Make up a mixture of equal parts glazing liquid and Patina Green glaze. Brush it randomly over the entire cover, blotting off some of it with a paper towel. I like the color to be a bit more concentrated in the corners. Brush on a mixture of Phthalo Green, Blue Shade and liquid glazing medium to intensify the color a bit.

12

Let the journal dry thoroughly. Apply tape to the back of all four sides of the metal piece so the sticky side is facing up.

13

Position the metal under the cutout window of the journal and press the cover to the tape to attach it.

14

Turn the cover over and burnish the tape well to the cover. Cut a piece of paste paper or decorative paper to a size just slightly smaller than the dimension of the front cover. Adhere the paper to the inside of the cover using gel medium. Adhere a second piece of paper to the inside of the back cover to complete.

VISIT CREATEMIXEDMEDIA.COM/ADVENTURES-IN-MIXED-MEDIA FOR BONUS CONTENT.

Make It!

CHARTING THE COURSE
LOOKING BACK SO WE CAN GO FORWARD

What's the first thing you can do with your Book of Dreams Journal? Begin by answering these questions.

1 When you look back, how do you honestly feel about the last year of your life? Where were you successful? What were your life or business challenges? (Personal, financial, etc.)

2 What are your creative and personal strengths?

3 When have you been honored and valued for doing what you truly love?

4 Name three specific areas of your life or business you would like to impact by using this book.

5 If you were completely honest with yourself, what limiting or false belief might be holding you back from stepping into your dreams?

6 Imagine that I have given you a magic wand; it has the capacity to remove all your fear and doubt. Close your eyes, wave the wand and presto: You are free! Now that you truly believe your dreams are obtainable, what will you reach for this year?

7 Are you ready for the creative adventure of a lifetime?

"IN THE SILENCE BETWEEN YOUR HEARTBEATS HIDES A SUMMONS . . . DO YOU HEAR IT?"

DREAMS AND VISIONING

Where am I going?
How do I get there?

What do you want to be when you grow up? This is a question that we ask kids when they're little. But how many adults have actually grown up to be what they dreamt about as children? We all have hopes and dreams for a rewarding and prosperous future. Did we grow up to be what we wanted to be? Or are will still dreaming? It seems like we start out chasing our dreams but end up accumulating a lot of stuff because our family, our friends, the media and big companies all have dreams for us as well. We say to ourselves, "One day when the kids are grown, the debts are paid and the stars align just right, then I'll start living my dream." But why wait? Start making the plans and laying the groundwork to grow those dreams into a reality. Fill your journal with the ideas and intentions that will grow and bloom throughout your life.

MATERIALS LIST

art journal

Chartpak Blender marker

label maker (optional)

pens of your choice

photocopies of images

photographs

string or yarn

GATHER YOUR FORCES: IMAGES OF INTENTION—EVIDENCE OF PERSONAL GROWTH AND DREAMS

If we stop growing, we must be dead. So start gathering the evidence of your growth and your dreams as you begin collecting fodder for the month because evolving into the people we dream of being is a difficult process. Be sure to look out for things that speak directly to your dreams and resonate with your spirit. Find articles online, in magazines or in newspapers. Perhaps there are images that can represent and symbolize your dreams. Maybe you aspire to be like someone, so find images of that person. Perhaps you dream of taking a class, shifting careers or traveling to a special place, so collect information, brochures and pamphlets. Save the catalog from your local community center or adult education program, or request a catalog from an art center like Penland School of Crafts or Arrowmont School of Arts and Crafts. There are many classes and opportunities out there. What are you dreaming of doing?

Whatever you gather, try to focus on things that you can do and not on the material things that you want. Stuff is easy to get, but experiences are unique and special. You can begin to set your intention by assembling these images of your dreams and beginning to interact and use them.

DREAMS AND VISIONING
from *Journal Fodder 365* by Eric M. Scott and David R. Modler

VISIT CREATEMIXEDMEDIA.COM/ADVENTURES-IN-MIXED-MEDIA FOR BONUS CONTENT.

STRATEGIC PLANNING

In order to attain your goals, you need to acknowledge and verbalize your dreams, and analyze the reality and feasibility of each one. Enlarge and clarify the dreams so that you can develop the strategies and the courage to make them happen. Start living the dream instead of dreaming to live.

Writing Prompt 1: Dream Journal

What are you dreaming about? We all have dreams, actual night visions that dance through our sleeping minds, as well as our hopes and aspirations. Document both kinds of dreams. Keep your journal, or at least some paper, next to your bed, and when you wake throughout the night or first thing in the morning, jot down your dreams before you forget them. Elaborate on these visions, and reflect on their contents and meanings. Keep pen and paper close at hand during the day, and write down your dreams, your hopes and your aspirations. Reflect on these thoughts and musings. This type of documentation becomes fertile soil for your intentions. What are you dreaming about at night when you sleep? What are the details and the nuances of the dreams? Do you have recurrent dreams? What are you dreaming about when you are awake? What are those aspirations? What do you dream about and hope for?

Writing Prompt 2: Daydreams

What thoughts, ideas and scenarios flash through your mind throughout the day? Our thoughts can very easily float away from us. We may be sitting in a meeting, and our minds may wander because the meeting doesn't hold our attention. We may daydream as we drive to work or to the store, or we may just sit and think, allowing thoughts and ideas to come and go at will. Pay attention to these times, and record and embrace these meanderings of the mind. They seem like whims, but they are peeks and glimpses into what we want and need the most. Pay attention to the fleeting thoughts that pop up throughout your day, and document them so that you don't forget. Where does your mind go when it isn't actively engaged? What are your daydreams? Do they hold clues about your bigger dreams and hopes?

Writing Prompt 3: Dreams and Nightmares

What do you fear most about trying to achieve your dreams? Along with dreams come nightmares. These may be nightmares that we have while sleeping, or the worst-case scenarios that we experience when we are awake. For many of us, it is impossible to imagine our dreams without imagining the nightmare. We think of all the reasons why it won't and can't work out. We balk at the fear, trip ourselves up and hold ourselves back. Acknowledge your dreams and nightmares, and shine light into your darkness. Don't let the possible nightmares squelch your dreams. Confront the negativity as a means to overcome it and move beyond it. What are your dreams? What are the corresponding nightmares? What are your worst-case scenarios? How can you overcome your nightmares?

Writing Prompt 4: Visions of Myself

Do you see yourself living your dream or living a life of want, longing and regret? A synonym of the word *dream* is *vision*. Often our vision of ourselves can directly affect whether or not we achieve our dreams. We have a clear picture in our minds of ourselves, but unfortunately that picture is often distorted by self-talk, doubts, fears and personal mythologies. Interrogate these visions of yourself to see if they hold up to scrutiny. Stop getting in your own way, and start visualizing yourself living the life you dream about. How do you see yourself? What can you do to see yourself in a more honest and authentic light? How could a clearer, truer vision of yourself help move you toward that dream?

WRITING TECHNIQUES

As you reflect on ways to live your dreams, create a mind map as a visual way to brainstorm and organize your thoughts and to begin developing a plan. The key to the mind map is to start with an overarching idea, and to branch out with different and more specific information as you go. Although this central idea is often and predictably placed in the center of a page, don't be afraid to span a two-page spread or place it anywhere you wish, like in a corner or at the bottom. As you branch out with your specific themes, use symbols and key phrases to represent your ideas. Your mind map can be as visually plain or elaborate as you wish. Use color and embellishments to create emphasis and to transform your map into a visual experience.

MIND MAPS

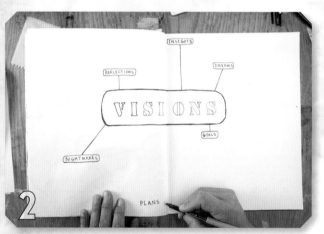

Write the word that you want to explore in the middle of the paper. You may want to draw a rectangle or oval around the word.

Brainstorm other words that you associate with your chosen word. Write these words around your first word. You may want to draw ovals and/or rectangles around these words. Connect these words to your original word with lines.

Brainstorm other words that you associate with your chosen word. Write these words around your first word. You may want to draw ovals and/or rectangles around these words. Connect these words to your original word with lines.

LABEL MAKER

It can be effective to quantify your hopes and place a label on your dreams. This labeling can be more than a figure of speech because you can use an actual label. A label maker isn't ideal for writing large chunks of text, but it is an easy way to call attention to those operative words and phrases that need some emphasis. Whether you have a simple handheld embossing label maker or a deluxe electronic one, explore the possibilities of using a label maker to create words and phrases. The embossing label maker that presses letters into plastic tape even creates a tactile sensation as the raised letters add actual texture and dimension to your page. But don't rush out and buy one if you don't have one. Think instead of how you might otherwise create labels and incorporate them into your pages.

Painting: Symmetrical String Designs

Like seeing images in the shapes of clouds, we often see something emerge from a random line, paint splotch or juxtaposed shape. Similar to the way inkblot tests help gain insight into someone's personality, we gain insight into our own hopes and dreams as we tap into our subconscious, allowing visions to emerge from the lines, colors and shapes we place on a page. We may begin to see our dreams more clearly, or our nightmares may begin to manifest from the resulting imagery. Whether these techniques give you glimpses into your subconscious or are just fun visual games to play, they open up new possibilities for dreaming in the journal.

1

Create a large pool of paint on a palette, and place a long piece of string into it so that it soaks up the paint. Or you can paint the string. Just make sure that the string is saturated with paint. Carefully place the string on the paper, allowing the ends of the string to stick out over the edge of the page.

2

Close your journal and gently hold it closed with your hand on top of it.

3

Pull on one or both ends of the string. You may need to get a hand from someone so that you can hold the journal closed and pull the string out at the same time.

INKED BACKGROUNDS, HAND LETTERING FROM GUEST ARTIST AIMEE DOLICH

I've been hand lettering off and on for twenty years. I love the way it feels to shape a letter into being—it almost feels like carving to me. Pairing that with my writing has been another breakthrough in my own style. I love to write. But until the last couple of years, it never occurred to me to hand letter my own poems and thoughts; I always lettered someone else's quotes.

With two little girls in my charge, my schedule is usually on their clock, so creative time is limited. If I can get it together and use that time efficiently, that restriction actually can work in my favor. I have to get creative about being creative.

I am slowly training myself to do much of my creative play when I'm not actually making something. My doodles nearly always start with words, and I've found those words flow best while I'm driving. I keep a notebook in my car and my bag, and when I finally get to a stoplight or a parking lot, I scribble like a maniac in that book. When I have a spare chunk of time, my ideas are there, and I can get right to work on the lettering and drawing.

Longer stretches of time turn anti-creative on me very quickly. Unless I'm thoroughly immersed in a project, I have to break up big blocks of time into smaller chunks to keep myself on track, or I drift and dwell and waste time.

I start with things that amuse me or grab me unexpectedly: conversations in our household, things my children do, my ever-changing moods, overheard comments in public and so on. I'm fascinated by what goes on in other people's heads. I love finding remnants of human activity and wondering what prompts people to do what they do. I live in a college town where odd things are always going on. It's hard not to be inspired in a place where such an independent spirit thrives.

In the past, I compartmentalized everything, and I nearly always ran into a dead end because it was a very unsatisfying way to go about making art. My attempts at acrylic, watercolor, lettering, writing and craft projects were all isolated attempts—nothing crossed the borders of the others. I focused solely on technique and the end product instead of enjoying the process. I've let that all go. Now everything blends together, and it feels much more authentic to create.

My lettering is all freehand. I pencil it out beforehand on my pre-inked backgrounds. Often I change my mind while I'm inking it in and change direction. I've found that the uneven, erratic style comes more naturally to me than traditional calligraphy; I can't get that kind of precision no matter how hard I practice. This is actually what I adore about hand lettering: You can put a pen in the hand of a hundred different people and tell them to letter the same word, and every result will be different.

I letter on paper, usually with black fine-tip Micron pens and sometimes with Rapidographs. Even though my fonts are uneven, I like a lot of control over my line. But you can use lots of different tools for hand lettering. Mine is one of many ways.

The concept of art seemed elusive and repressive to me for a long time because I focused constantly on what I didn't know or didn't have. When I realized I didn't have to look outside of myself to find my own style, I started to truly enjoy creating.

AIMEE DOLICH: INKED BACKGROUNDS AND HAND LETTERING
from *The Artist Unique* by Carmen Torbus

AIMEE'S INKED BACKGROUNDS, STEP BY STEP

For my backgrounds, I use mostly ink pads—any kind, ranging from inexpensive dye to lush pigment inks, dry to saturated. It is a quick, easy way to get a burst of color that requires virtually no prep.

This technique will work on anything that absorbs ink. Try it on untreated canvas, wood, ribbon, envelopes and picture frame mats. In most cases, you can brush on a layer of acrylic finish so the color won't fade.

MATERIALS LIST

art journal

crayons (optional)

ink pad

large scrap paper

pens of your choice

watercolor paints

watercolor paintbrushes

they SAY you can't go BACK • but THERE are ALWAYS exceptions and THIS was ONE of them • So i Returned TO FIND that PIECE of MY IDENTITY that I should have NEVER abandoned • it was JUST where I had Left IT • CONFUSED and A BIT resentful FoR being DESERTED • but most IMPORTANTLY ALIVE • and Eager FOR the Rest of the JOURNEY

TIPS

• For journal pages, I use Moleskine blank notebooks. For illustrations and bigger lettering projects, I use hot-pressed paper, which has a smooth finish and prevents ink from bleeding.

• Sometimes I use watercolor instead of, or in addition to, the ink pads to color my backgrounds. I also use gouache, a thick and opaque paint, because I like the way it contrasts with the bright background ink colors and because it covers up my goofs.

1. Put a piece of paper underneath your background paper. This will protect your work surface. Colors will spill onto that overflow paper, which you can then cut up and use for collage.

2. Turn the ink pad upside down and start rubbing it over your surface. Drier ink pads work best for cloudy effects; wetter ink pads are good for deep, saturated color.

3. Try various application methods. Touch lightly on your paper to capture the patterns and imperfections of the ink pad surface. Draw lines with the edges. Put crayon or wax resists underneath the inking to create texture. Combine it with watercolor. There really are no limits to this technique.

IDENTITY
Aimee Dolich
Gouache and ink on paper
11" × 8½" (28cm × 22cm)

HAND LETTERING

Your handwriting is uniquely yours. So why not use it to create artwork that is unique, too? A smooth surface makes lettering easier, so keep that in mind if you want to add hand lettering to your artwork. On a textured background, use a pen or marker that will work well on the texture. On paper, results will vary depending on the tool, so proceed by trial and error. I love adding drippy inked text to my collage paintings using India ink and a dip pen. You could also try using a small paintbrush with thin acrylic paint or paint pens.

MATERIALS LIST

Hand-lettering tools and mediums of your choice

Substrate of your choice

VISIT CREATEMIXEDMEDIA.COM/ADVENTURES-IN-MIXED-MEDIA FOR BONUS CONTENT.

1

2

This is the type of lettering I use most frequently in my artwork: drippy ink letters. Get a lot of ink on your pen (the more ink, the messier the result). Go slowly as you write your word; you can always go back over it if you need to. Put some pools of ink where you'd like to encourage it to drip.

Tilt the piece straight up, tap it and allow the ink to drip. Then lay it down flat to dry.

1

2

Draw letters.

Embellish them any way you want.

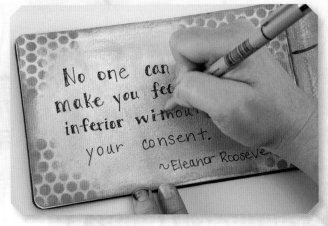

These began as printed letters. I went back with a pen and doodled up the left edges of their strokes.

SCRAPED AND PAINTED BACKGROUNDS

I love to scrape paint onto my pages. When you scrape paint, you can get very thin layers that overlap and play with one another to create lots of intensity. One reason I use this technique often is that I hate to waste paint on my palette. If I have extra paint, I will pick it up with a scraper and put it on a blank journal page (or on two or three). I let the paint dry and come back to it later, sometimes even months later. The scraped paint is always a nice surprise and provides a simple starting layer for a new page.

I used it to create continuance in the background while the rubbed stencil imagery leads the eye around the page.

MATERIALS LIST

12" × 12" (30cm × 30cm) canvas

acrylic paint-Sky Blue Light, Medium Magenta, Indian Yellow Hue, Payne's Grey, Titanium White

adhesive

black spray paint or black acrylic paint

cotton rag

gel medium

gesso

large image of a person from a fashion magazine

old book pages

old gift card for scraping

palette knife

permanent black ink pad

scissors

sewing machine and black thread

stencil (raindrop)

watercolor paper

white pen

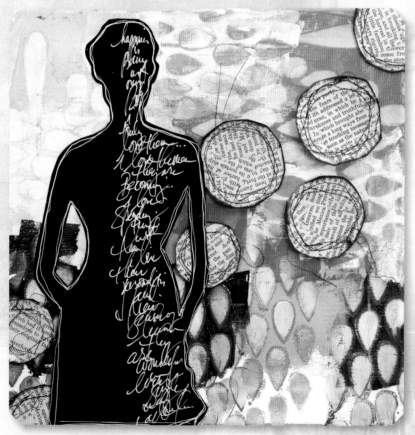

SCRAPED AND PAINTED BACKGROUNDS
from *Art Journal Freedom* by Dina Wakley

acrylic paint (Amsterdam, Golden); adhesive (Tombow); gel medium (Liquitex); gesso (Dick Blick); ink pad (Archival by Ranger); spray paint (Krylon); poster paint pen (Sharpie); stencil (Crafter's Workshop); watercolor paper (Canson)

VISIT CREATEMIXEDMEDIA.COM/ADVENTURES-IN-MIXED-MEDIA FOR BONUS CONTENT.

1

Coat your canvas with a thin coat of white gesso and let it dry. Scrape some light blue paint onto the top left area of the canvas. A little paint goes a long way.

2

Scrape some magenta paint onto the top right area of the canvas. Overlap the magenta and the light blue slightly.

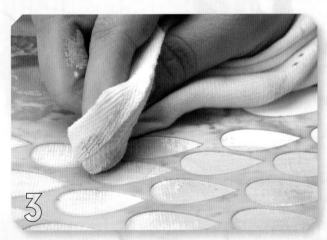

3

Place a stencil over your painted areas. Use a damp rag to rub through the stencil and remove some of the paint. This takes a little pressure—don't be afraid of pressing hard. Remove some of the paint from both the blue area and the magenta area. Turn the stencil with each color so the pattern goes in different directions.

4

Scrape some yellow paint below the magenta area. Use the damp rag and the stencil to remove some of the yellow paint. As you remove paint, the rag will get dirty. You can use the paint on the rag to add some stenciling below the yellow paint.

5

Scrape some gray paint onto the canvas over three small areas. Don't be afraid to scrape it right over the other colors.

6

Scrape some white paint onto the canvas over three small areas. Again, layer the white over other colors and layers.

7

Use the damp rag and the stencil to remove some of the white paint. Each time you add some paint and remove some of it through the stenciling, you add visual complexity and texture to your background. The scraped colors overlap and interact with each other.

Let all of your paint layers dry completely.

8

Use gel medium and a palette knife to cover a sheet of watercolor paper with pieces of torn book paper. Be sure to put gel both on top and on the back of each piece of paper. Scrape any excess gel from the top of the book paper so there are no globs. Let the gel dry.

9

10

Cut out some freehand circles from the paper. I don't worry about the circles being perfect. I like them to be wonky!

Ink the edges of the circles with permanent black ink. Inking collage elements can help them stand out from a busy background.

Sew around the circles with black thread. I love the added texture that sewing provides. I have an obsession with leaving my threads loose and untrimmed, too.

11

12

Cut a silhouette from a fashion magazine. Paint the silhouette black with spray paint or acrylic paint. Let it dry.

When the paint is dry, use a white pen to outline the silhouette and add journaling. To make sure your white paint pen is nice and opaque, shake it for at least 60 seconds.

Glue the book page circles and silhouette onto your canvas.

Make It!

MARK MAKING

The way that you make a mark is as individual as the way you write your signature. The tools that you use become an extension of your arm just as with the paintbrush.

MATERIALS LIST

acrylic paint

art journal or other substrate

fluid acrylics

variety of mark-making tools

MARK MAKING
from *Mixed Media Painting Workshop*
by Jean Pederson

An Array of Tools to Play With

You can use anything that you don't mind getting paint on to make marks. I raid the garage and pick up interesting things at yard sales and hardware stores. Nothing is off limits to me with regard to tools for making marks in a painting. Once I have a pile of tools I will play around with the objects, holding them in different ways, rolling, rocking, scraping, dragging them across the wet painted surface.

Have fun. Practice making marks using the tools as stamps, using brushes loaded with paint, using sticks to make lines. Notice the variety offered with different pressures, different techniques.

Once you have experimented with the various tools at your disposal, think about where those marks might look good. What application will you use for your next landscape or still life? Would the marks be best for an abstract image or a referential one?

VISIT CREATEMIXEDMEDIA.COM/ADVENTURES-IN-MIXED-MEDIA FOR BONUS CONTENT.

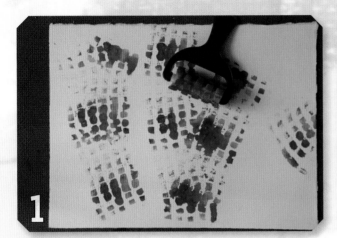

1

This is a roller I purchased at the local hardware store. It's interesting to see the mechanical and somewhat predictable marks it makes.

2

Stencils are a great tool for making marks and also for communicating ideas through their symbolism. I used *J* for obvious reasons! I found a nut attached to a bolt and stamped and rolled it on the paper with Teal fluid acrylics.

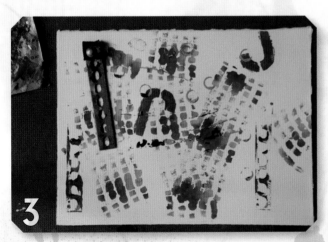

3

I have no idea what this is, but I found it in the garage and it makes great mechanical lines!

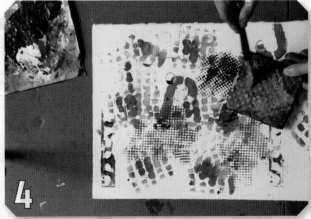

4

The foam plate from yesterday's steak dinner and a no-skid pad for the sink make great gridded dots.

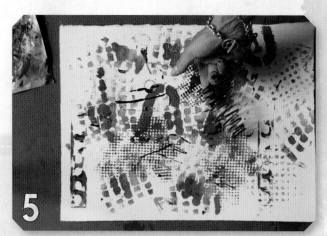

I dragged this old spring through my palette and rolled it onto the surface of the paper.

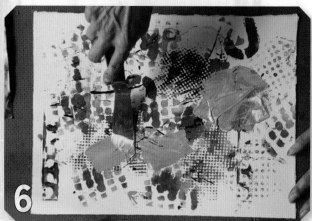

Trowels and palette knives are very useful for making larger marks and shapes. In this example I applied a more viscous paint with a trowel. I then scraped back some of the paint, also with a trowel.

Tools from other disciplines are useful in painting. I have a bunch of ceramics tools that have come in handy for the wonderful marks they provide. Notice how the scraping tools expose the obscured patterns from the thick opaque paint.

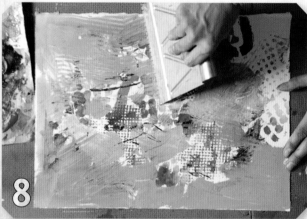

Go big! Try adding more paint over patterned areas and then scrape it back with a large serrated trowel. Notice that the paint is opaque and thick.

VISIT CREATEMIXEDMEDIA.COM/ADVENTURES-IN-MIXED-MEDIA FOR BONUS CONTENT.

Go small! I found a stick in the garden to use for scraping in calligraphic lines.

I used a large palette knife to spread and scrape paint onto the surface.

Any kind of flocked material is great for stamping patterns onto your surface. The flocking can also be used to lift paint off your surface. I used a flocked gift bag that I picked up on sale at the local bookstore.

Your finished ground might look something like this. Remember, there are no rules except to trust your intuition and have fun with the process.

EVERY FACE TELLS A STORY

PAINTED FACE VALUE STUDY

Every face is defined by its shape and skin tone, the size, color and sparkle of the eyes; the texture of hair or absence of it; the changing shape of the mouth; the rose in the cheek; or untold stories etched in silent wrinkles. The face is also a vehicle for expressing emotion. We need not utter a sound; the eyes alone are a window to the soul.

In this project you will be experimenting with contrast using both collage and paint to create a face. The idea is NOT to reproduce the face you started with but to use this face as a value guide to inspire you to paint a unique face of your own. You will build light and shadow with various colors; however, the color itself isn't as important as the value. An easy way to determine value is to squint at something.

When you find yourself "in the flow" as you create, follow the lead of your intuition: experiment, deviate, take a chance. If you get lost, you can always come back to the original print and come back into your painting with line and contrast.

MATERIALS LIST

140-lb. (300gsm) watercolor paper

acrylic paints, assorted colors, including "face colors": Phthalo Blue, Naphthol Red Light, Hansa Yellow Medium, Titanium White, Quinacridone Crimson, Quinacridone Nickel Azo Gold, Payne's Gray and black

black-and-white photocopy of a face, such as one from a magazine

carbon paper

collage paper scraps

dull no. 2 pencil

paintbrushes

palette paper

razor blade

rubbing alcohol

scissors

soft cloth

soft gel medium

Stabilo pencil

tape

tracing paper or deli wrap

water container (to rinse brushes)

white gel pen

white gesso

EVERY FACE TELLS A STORY
from *Layered Impressions* by Katie Kendrick

Expression Direction

Look into a mirror, staring into your own eyes, examining your face, for at least two minutes. Make mental notes of thoughts and emotions that arise. Afterwards, write down a column of words or short phrases to represent observations about your experience. Here are a few questions to get you started: Describe the eyes that looked back at you. What is the mouth saying, even when it is closed? Does the reflection seem happy, sad, scared, peaceful or . . . ? What secrets does the mirror reveal about you that you find difficult to see?

Circle ten of these words and phrases and compose a "self-portrait" poem with them. Make sure to write the date on it. Repeat this exercise once a day for a week and notice the variations you discover, if there are any.

1 Gather small pieces of various collage papers and separate them into piles of light, medium and dark. Cutting up magazine pages works well for this.

2 Find a face you like with defined contrast, mainly light and dark areas with a minimum of grays. Use a photo-editing program to convert your picture to black-and-white with high contrast. Print out a copy about the same size as your paper. Tape it to a piece of watercolor paper with a piece of carbon paper sandwiched between it and the watercolor paper. Use a dull pencil to trace over primary lines that separate the light and dark areas. You're not trying to reproduce every line, just the general form.

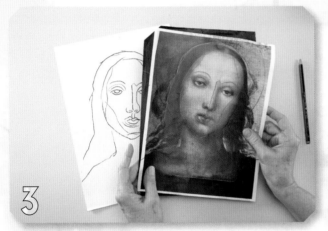

3 Remove the carbon paper and face image.

4 Using gel medium, begin gluing down pieces of paper to the face, using the original face print as a guide for the placement of the light, medium and dark papers. Use a razor blade over the paper to work out any air bubbles trapped in the glue. It's fine to let the paper pieces overlap lines and into other areas. You can use a Stabilo or graphite pencil to retrace lines when necessary.

5 Set up your palette with your paints. I recommend using two blues: Payne's Gray and Phthalo Blue; two reds: Quinacridone Crimson and Naphthol Red Light; two yellows: Quinacridone Nickel Azo Gold and Hansa Yellow Medium; Titanium White; and a black.

HOMEMADE PALETTE PAD

For a cheap and easy homemade palette pad, cut a dozen pieces of freezer paper and, with the shiny side up, staple them together. Tape the stack to a slightly larger cardboard base using duct tape. Use a piece of removable duct tape at the bottom of the page to keep the paper from curling.

Pick up a small amount of each red and yellow on your brush and mix them together. Then add a tiny bit of the blue. This combination gives you a dark value flesh tone that can be tweaked warmer or cooler by adding a touch more of the yellow, red or blue.

Paint the dark value flesh tone on areas of the painting that you see as dark.

After the darks are laid down, add a little white to the mix to create a medium flesh tone.

Paint this medium tone onto the face in what would be the gray areas of your painting. This is not precision paint-by-number painting. It helps to have a bit of a slapdash attitude when putting down paint.

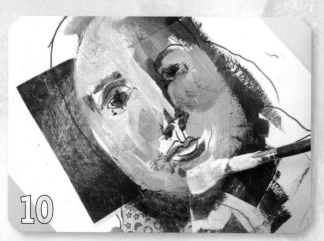

To add rosy tones to the face, mix a tiny bit of red to the dark flesh tone and apply it to the cheeks and lips. Pick up additional white, mix it into the flesh tone and start adding some light areas.

Continue adding whitened highlights to the areas that need it, using the original art as a guide.

VISIT CREATEMIXEDMEDIA.COM/ADVENTURES-IN-MIXED-MEDIA FOR BONUS CONTENT.

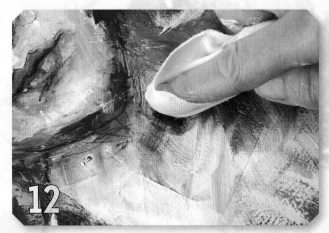

12

To reveal elements of collage paper that may get buried under paint, use the tip of a soft cloth soaked in rubbing alcohol and rub the area gently to lift off some of the paint.

13

For the finishing line-work details, use a Stabilo pencil to detail the pupils, lids and other areas of the eyes. A white gel pen works well to add a highlight to the pupils.

14

Detail the nose and lips in this way as well. Gently smear a line with your finger if it appears too bold.

15

Continue working the face, head and just hints of the torso, keeping in mind that it's not necessary to add in every last detail.

For the background behind the head, paint the area with a layer of white gesso and then add the color(s) of your choice. If you're unsure of what color to use, identify a prominent color in the painting and select its complement (the color opposite it on the color wheel) to make your painting "pop."

BENEATH THE LAYERS

If you're unsure of a background color, trace the silhouette of the figure onto tracing paper or deli wrap and then use it as a template on watercolor paper. Apply different colors to the watercolor paper and hold it up to the painting to try the colors out.

USING TEA BAGS

Old, dried tea bags can add magic to your artwork. It's no joke. Each tea bag has a different pattern of staining. Some tea stains are subtle, while others are more obvious. Tea bags containing berry teas are particular favorites of mine due to their rich crimson stains. I use tea bags to create an aged look, to mute a too-bright color and to add texture. I like to tear off the telltale edges of the tea bags before I use them. Once they're on a piece, they won't look like tea bags at all, but rather like a mysterious vintage surface. In this project you'll get to play with this inventive technique.

MATERIALS LIST

acrylic paint—Buff, Green Turquoise, Nickel Azo Gold, transparent Red Iron Oxide, red, sky blue

glaze medium

paintbrushes

paper towel

pre-gessoed wood panel, canvas or canvas boards

scissors

used tea bags, dried

vintage book pages and newspaper

watercolor crayon

Casa de las Palabras
Mixed media on board

USING TEA BAGS
from *Wabi-Sabi Art Workshop*
by Serena Barton

VISIT CREATEMIXEDMEDIA.COM/ADVENTURES-IN-MIXED-MEDIA FOR BONUS CONTENT.

1

Using a pre-gessoed panel, canvas or canvas board, paint a layer of Green Turquoise acrylic paint over the top of the piece.

2

Paint a layer of Buff acrylic paint over the bottom of the piece.

3

Collage a variety of text: pieces from vintage books, newspapers and dictionary pages. Use pages that have small illustrations on them.

4

Paint a layer of Nickel Azo Gold paint and glaze medium over the entire piece and blot it. When the gold layer is dry, add a layer of transparent Red Iron Oxide paint and glaze medium. Wipe the area lightly with a paper towel.

**NEW YEAR'S DAY—
THE SOUND OF WATER
FROM A CREEK.**
—Raizan

5 Mix some Red Iron Oxide with gel medium and paint an uneven horizontal line above the text area.

6 Take a dry used tea bag and cut off the top under the staple. If you have a lot of patience you can remove the staple with needle-nosed pliers instead. Open up the tea bag at the seam and empty the tea into a container. Repeat with other tea bags as needed. Collage the tea bags and torn pieces over the top area of the piece. Look for interesting tea stains to include.

7 With a small brush, dash down a small area of bright red acrylic paint on the line across the piece.

8 Brush on a short line of sky blue paint below the red area.

9

Handwrite text in the upper gold area with a watercolor crayon. Rub gently to partially obscure the text.

Teahouse

Encaustic and collage on found wood panel

I used part of an old shelf for this piece's support. You can find interesting wood like this at recycling and reuse stores, garage sales or even in a free pile outside a secondhand store. Used tea bags form the "house" in this stylized mixed-media piece.

UNEARTH YOUR ARTISTIC ADVENTURER

In this section, you will look at how you can use your words and photos to inspire a mixed-media creation. I invite you to read about contributor Kelly Barton's experience walking through these prompts in mediums she is not as comfortable with before heading into her studio to create in the environment where she feels more at ease. Maybe you will be inspired to create a collage or another mixed-media piece that represents where you are as you begin this journey toward the inner you.

KELLY BARTON

When I talked to Kelly Barton about creating a mixed-media piece for this chapter, I asked if she might be open to following poetry and photography prompts as a starting point before creating her painting. Her response was something along the lines of, "You want me to write a poem? I do not write poetry." I loved this response. She patiently listened as I explained what I meant. A word list. Stringing those words together as the beginnings of a poem. "I could totally do that," she said.

Kelly started with the poetry prompt of taking a book down from her bookshelf and writing a word list. She then used the words to create this poem:

i am me . . .

me, patchouli, sunny, tiny bewigged, me
warhol factory silly betty creative, me
to be uninhibited, authentic, fearless
me. glamorous outsider, resilient, free.

In the past few months, Kelly has begun to play with self-portrait photography. She has made it a goal to learn more about how to use her camera and which lens works best for the moments she wants to capture. When I asked her to take a series of photos, she was drawn to take several mirror self-portraits that represent different emotions and moods she experienced throughout one day.

UNEARTHING YOUR ARTISTIC ADVENTURER
from *Inner Excavation* by Liz Lamoreux

Artwork by Kelly Barton

Although the poem and the photos are not directly part of the mixed-media painting, the experience of taking the photos and writing the poem influenced the mood Kelly created in this piece. She pulled the word "free" from her poem and used it in her painting to illustrate the idea of simply being herself and being true to the person she is. She pushed herself to let go of her preconceived notions of self-portraits as well as of herself. Through her artwork, she expresses what she learned from this experience, which is part of the freedom she feels when she creates.

ARTIST ILLUMINATION
INTERVIEW WITH KELLY BARTON

Here is a glimpse into how Kelly sees herself.

Who are you?

i am
　　a frida-loving
　　　sassy irish maiden

a silly inappropriate creative

　　a brave warrior girl

sunny betty laughter

　　i am a gypsy
　　　life explorer

i am
　　beloved. free. girl.

Who or what inspires you?

Books/Authors:
The Prophet *by Kahlil Gibran*
I was just introduced to the poet David Whyte. When his poem "Sweet Darkness" was read to me, I simply felt: Home.

Music:
"Redemption Song" by Bob Marley

How do you nurture yourself?
Kelly + Nurture = Nap!

How did you find your creative voice?
I feel like she (my creative voice) has always been there, but after years of ignoring her, the gypsy decided it was long overdue and she needed to come out and play. Pretty happy she did!

Kelly's response to "Who are you?"

IN THE STUDIO: A COLLAGE OF YOU

This is your permission slip to begin creating a piece of art inspired by your words and photos.

Task: Create a mixed-media collage using photos you have taken and text you have written.

Notes: You might want to simply use the photos and text as inspiration or you might want to add them directly into your collage.

Other things to consider:
- Is there an art medium you've wanted to play with but haven't?
- How might you incorporate your words and photos into a medium you already feel comfortable with?
- If the idea of "choosing" an art medium seems over-whelming, try this: Give yourself the gift of a new box of crayons, a blank unlined journal, some glue and a few new fun pens. Print out your chosen photos. Begin to simply have fun with these tools as you create with your own words, images and color.

Tools for the Journey:
Kelly's Collage Tips

A few ideas to get you started with collage:

Substrate: Decide what you will use as the base for your collage. You might begin with a standard canvas or a piece of watercolor paper. However, you could also think outside the box and use an old wooden tray, a vintage frame, corrugated cardboard, scraps of wood or old book covers. (Note that gesso is a great way to prime your surface if needed.)

Collage Papers: Here are some of my favorite non-traditional paper sources: magazine pages, children's catalogs, food and beverage labels or pieces of mail.

Glue: I usually use gel medium. There are several out there (from glossy to matte); experiment to find the one that you like best. When you are creating just for fun, consider using a glue stick or regular white glue.

Paint and other mediums: What I love most about mixed media is the freedom to use different mediums within the same painting. I often use graphite for outlining and layering under the paint. A few paint options to think about:
- If you are just starting out, try craft acrylics. They are inexpensive and great to practice with (many experienced artists use them all the time).
- Liquitex and Golden brand paints are more expensive but have different textures and weights than the less expensive paints. The pigments and coverage can be richer as well.
- Many acrylic brands also carry complementary mediums such as molding paste, granulars and finishes. These can assist in layers and texturing.

Ready to start? Here are some thoughts:
- Collage your background with various papers, graphics and stamped images.
- Give the background a wash of color.
- Gel medium can be used to transfer photos (there are several tutorials on the Internet).
- Fabrics, ribbon and lace are perfect additions to backgrounds or finishing touches.

Don't forget: Allow yourself to create freely. Don't focus on how you "think" you have to do it. Experiment and enjoy the process.

DELVING INTO THE QUIET: A PERSONAL PRACTICE

Each day, I try to bring moments of quiet and ritual into my life. Many mornings, I begin the day with a cup of tea and a lit candle, then I write a few pages in my journal and then stretch and breathe my way into the day with a few yoga poses. When dusk arrives early in the fall and winter, I light candles throughout the house to bring in the light. While I light these candles, I think of people in my life and send out blessings to them. These moments are part of my personal practice and act as bookends to the ebb and flow of my days.

The quiet of these moments also invites a balance in my life. When I am writing just to let the thoughts escape my very chatty brain or stretching my body to awaken it, I am not running ahead to the next project, blog post, idea. When you are in the habit of pushing yourself to unearth the reasons and feelings behind where you are on your path, you also need to give yourself the gift of the quiet, the rest, the repetition of comfort and self-care.

I invite you to think about the things you already do that make up your personal practice. Maybe you write "morning pages" as prescribed by Julia Cameron in *The Artist's Way*. Maybe you go for a daily walk or take a break in the middle of the day with a book and a cup of tea. Perhaps you run or practice yoga. Think about what you already do that is part of your practice. Think about what you might like to add to a daily practice.

PAINTING WITHOUT PAINT

One of my favorite things about mixed-media artist Misty Mawn's work is her approach to color. I adore the limited palette and subtle hues she achieves in her white-on-white work. Inspired by her gorgeous painting, this project works with analogous colors in a most unusual way, without even touching paint.

Sounds crazy, right? Painting without paint? Laugh if you want, but I think you'll come to love this nontraditional process because it is much more forgiving than "real" painting. In fact, this is how I made most of my work before I became adept at mixing and managing paints. This project is reminiscent of a coloring book; it allows you to carve lines and then color in the spaces. The flexibility enables you to build lots of layers, but you can also go back and remove certain areas due to the unusual qualities inherent to Clayboard. Let's get started so you can see what I'm talking about.

MATERIALS LIST

- acrylic matte medium
- acrylic paint markers (DecoArt)
- airbrush paints
- cheese grater from dollar store
- Clayboard, smooth, flat panels, any size
- dental tools or any other hand-carving tools, such as those manufactured by Ampersand
- gesso
- hair dryer
- oil pastels
- paintbrushes
- PanPastels
- pencil
- soft pastels, a few monochromatic colors
- spray bottle of water
- wire brush

PAINTING WITHOUT PAINT
from *Flavor for Mixed Media* by Mary Beth Shaw

VISIT CREATEMIXEDMEDIA.COM/ADVENTURES-IN-MIXED-MEDIA FOR BONUS CONTENT.

1 Using a pencil, sketch out a rough composition on the Clayboard.

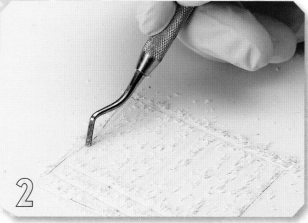

2 Pick a few areas and carve out some texture using one of any number of tools. Dental tools work really well.

3 A handheld cheese grater makes wonderful texture. I place the Clayboard on the edge of the table and hack at it with the grater, but do whatever works best for you.

4 Wire brushes come in a number of sizes and give you an interesting multiline texture. Experiment with tools and see what you like the best.

5

When you have completed creating texture, you are ready to begin adding the first layer of color using soft pastels. Pick several colors and color different areas of your piece. Note: Storing your pastels in rice flour will prevent colors from mixing with one another.

6

Put some gesso on your brush and work it into the pastels on the board. This is done with dabbing, stroking or scrubbing motions—try all three to see the difference in effect. Rinse your brush between colors. The gesso will blend and lighten the pastel. It will also fix the pastel into place on the Clayboard so it is no longer airborne.

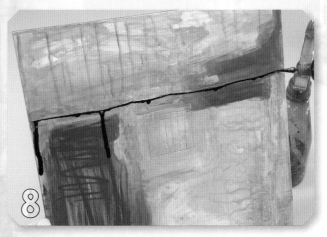

7

Alternatively you can use matte medium instead of gesso to fix the pastel without changing its color. Work matte medium gently over the areas where you want more intense color. Keep in mind that you don't need to create opaque blocks of color; the piece will actually be more interesting if there are value changes within each section. If you want the carved texture to show, be sure to work pastel into the recessed areas.

8

Using a contrasting color of airbrush paint, apply a line of color to the board, squeezing it directly from a bottle that has a tip on it.

9

Holding the board upright, spritz it with water to make the paint run.

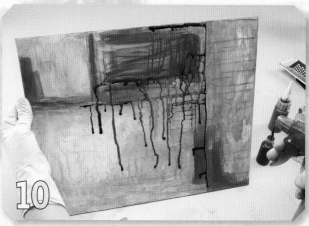

10

I like to turn the board once or twice to change the direction of the running paint.

11

Spritz again to make the ink drip more if desired. The more water you add, the more it will lighten the color of the ink.

12

A hair dryer can be used to alter or slow down the flow of the paint.

PAINTED PAPER TOWELS

I always always always keep a damp paper towel in my hand, especially when I am spritzing water and creating drips. You never know when you might want to dab here or there and pull back some color. Sometimes after spraying, I use just the very corner of the paper towel to absorb ink from an isolated area. I buy solid white paper towels and use the same one over and over, laying it out to dry at the end of each day. They are very pretty and quite useful for other projects.

13

After the piece is dry, add more depth to some of the carved areas using oil pastel. Work the pastel into an area using a cosmetic sponge or your gloved finger.

14

It's never too late to go back and create additional texture with your carving tools. This is a great way to add some white areas if desired.

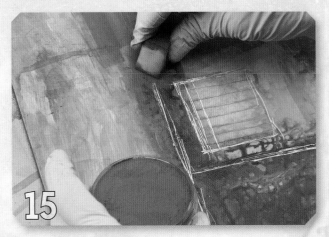

15

I use PanPastels to work on shadowing and add highlights in certain areas. The color is applied with a sponge and stays put better than soft pastels.

16

You can add pops of specific color or add linear detail with the acrylic paint markers. If you sort of "pounce" gently on the tip of the marker, it will create a splat on your piece that is often interesting.

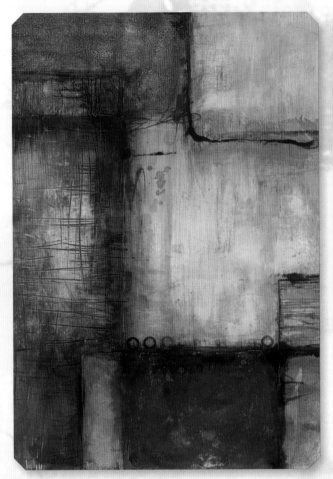

I started these pieces side by side, with a composition that spanned both pieces. During the process, I frequently turned them and worked in all four directions. Working abstract paintings this way can lead to more interesting results.

WHAT'S IN YOUR PANTRY?

No Clayboard? Don't despair; grab whatever substrate you have on hand such as watercolor paper or canvas. Simply skip over the carving part of the project and proceed as indicated. Another alternative is to substitute water-soluble pencils or crayons—even water-soluble oil pastels. Instead of blending the pencils with water, use matte medium. Or try wetting your paper first with matte medium (or gesso) and draw into it or sand bits of watercolor pencil over your wet substrate. Sprinkle with kosher salt.

3

REFINE YOUR STYLE, REPURPOSE YOUR ART

Now that you've mastered the basic mixed-media techniques and tried larger canvas artworks, it's time to take the next step in your adventure. Chances are, while you were practicing those basic techniques you created some pieces of art that maybe aren't your favorite. Perhaps they're a bit messy or just didn't turn out the way you planned. In this chapter, not only can you rescue those pieces from the trash can, you will refine your skills while you do so.

With techniques from mixed-media master artists like Mary Beth Shaw, Darlene Olivia McElroy, Sandra Duran Wilson and Kelly Rae Roberts, you'll use materials you've found or otherwise would have discarded. You'll think about mixed-media art in new ways and ultimately establish your own signature art style.

MAGAZINE MAGIC

The vast majority of my art is labor intensive. Paintings that I work over and over, alternatively struggling, rejoicing, repeating often for days and even months before all the layers are finished. I have often joked that a project isn't done until I have bled on it, as if I had to suffer for it to be right. This is not one of those projects.

This project uses stencils as rubbing plates underneath magazine pages. And it is indeed magical how quickly you can create a seemingly complex background. I selected my pages from decorating magazines and have found that some pages make better rubbings than others. Play around until you find out what works best for you.

These backgrounds are so fun and easy you'll find yourself tearing pages out of magazines and saving them for later use. In one work session, you can make a bunch of rubbings at a time to build a supply of collage elements.

MATERIALS LIST

acrylic paint

canvas board, mat board or any flat substrate

craft knife

gel medium or collage medium (such as Pam Carriker's Mixed Media Adhesive)

magazines

paintbrush

palette knife

sandpaper

screen-printing squeegee

stencils

Thermofax screen (optional)

Select some pages from a magazine. Lay a page on top of a stencil and sand the magazine paper lightly, using sandpaper. The outline of the stencil image will show through. Experiment with fine-grit and rougher sandpapers to see which effect you like best. Sand enough pages to create a series of horizontal strips that will go across the board.

MAGAZINE MAGIC
from *Stencil Girl* by Mary Beth Shaw

Mix up a background color that will coordinate with your magazine pages and paint the board. This is just in case your torn strips don't line up sufficiently.

3

Using gel medium or collage medium, adhere your sanded strips to the board.

4

Allow the collage to dry, then turn the board over and trim the excess paper from the edges with a craft knife.

5

Set your Thermofax screen over your collaged board. I chose a screen designed by Margaret Applin, but you can easily substitute a stencil. If you are using a screen, spread a thick line of fluid acrylic at the top of the screen. (I used Micaceous Iron Oxide) on the top edge as shown.

6

Pull the paint down over the screen using a screen-printing squeegee or other spreader.

7

Remove the Thermofax screen.

HERE'S A TIP

A Thermofax is like a small silkscreen except it's not silk; it is polyester. I consider them cousins to stencils. They are similar in that they allow the artist to create a repeated image over and over. They differ, though, because the Thermofax screen, by its nature, allows more detail than a stencil, so fine lines are better replicated. There are several places where you can buy ready-made screens and also where you can have your own images put onto screens. I have listed those in the Resources (CreateMixedMedia.com/stencilgirl). Use them alone or in combination with stencils.

Mixed-media artists are known to save everything from labels, old envelopes, magazines and scraps of paper to things we pick up off the street. Yep, ephemera. All that transitory written and printed matter not intended to be retained or preserved. Enter the mixed-media artists to reuse almost everything imaginable. Sometimes you may get carried away and glue everything down at once. If you end up with a busy background and need to tone it down or unify it, here are a few ways you can do so.

TECHNIQUE ONE: WASH IT

Tie all your elements together with a gesso wash or a paint wash.

MATERIALS LIST

- acrylic paint
- collage
- gesso
- matte gel medium
- paintbrush
- water
- white glue

1. Thin your gesso or paint with water to your desired consistency.

2. Paint a thin layer of watered-down gesso or paint over your dry collaged surface. One coat will usually do the job; you want the collage to show through.

3. Add interest to the gesso layer by splattering water on it, letting most of the water dry, and then blotting the remaining water.

TECHNIQUE TWO: FOG IT

Create a foggy surface over the collage and make it mysterious with a faux encaustic layer.

1. Spread a layer of matte gel over the surface of your ephemera-collaged surface. When the gel is dry, you can continue to work the surface as desired.

TECHNIQUE THREE: CRACKLE IT

Give your art a crackle finish that allows you to see the layers underneath.

Spread a layer of white craft glue over your dried collaged surface.

While the glue is still wet, paint acrylic paint onto the glue. Do not mix the paint into the glue—just float a layer of paint on top of the glue.

The glue and paint will crackle when they dry, and you will be able to see your collage through the cracks.

TIPS

- Are you afraid of wrecking your collage background? You can add an isolation coat of clear polymer medium before you try these techniques. Let the polymer medium dry completely. If you don't like the outcome, you can wipe it off and you will have your original background. You may also spray it with rubbing alcohol to remove the paint, gesso or faux encaustic.
- These techniques can be seen in greater detail in *Surface Treatment Workshop*.

BE GREEN
from *Mixed Media Revolution* by Darlene Olivia McElroy and Sandra Duran Wilson

OBSCURED COLLAGE

In this demonstration, you'll practice drawing and painting an image superimposed over a collaged support, integrating mixed media into an image. Instead of a completely covered surface this surface is only partially covered with lots of blank space within the original design of the collage. It is important that you look at the surface as a blank surface with nothing on it and draw your image over what is there despite the collage. Resist the temptation to see referential imagery in the collaged pieces.

MATERIALS LIST

collage paper

collaged surface

fluid acrylics-Quinacridone Gold, Quinacridone Magenta, Phthalo Blue

matte medium

pencil

pencil crayon, black

paintbrushes appropriate for your chosen paints and mediums

OBSCURED COLLAGE
from *Mixed Media Painting Workshop* by Jean Pederson

Behind the Eyes

11" × 11" (28cm × 28cm), collage and acrylic on cradled board, collection of Mr. L. Bogdon

Use your opaque paint to push around your lights and darks. Here I added a veil of semi-opaque tinted white gesso on the right side of the face and some black tinted gesso on the left. My intention was to create form, so I continued to build colors and value to achieve this look.

You can also use a black pencil crayon to infuse line into the imagery. Or, while the paint is still wet, try scraping some of it away to create variations of line and value.

When you use a combination of collaged pieces, mediums and paint, the result is an uneven surface with one medium accepting paint differently than another medium. These imperfections appeal to me because the result is a richer surface.

Go back to your previous collage exercises and choose one of them as your surface.

Choose a subject and draw your image with a pencil. Consider what your priority is in regard to the elements of design. My priority here is value and source of light in creating form. Thus I draw in all my light, middle and dark shapes. Remember to draw through the collage pieces as though they are not there.

Start with a transparent paint. You can thin it with a bit of water and matte medium if necessary.

Brush on layers of gold, blue and magenta in different combinations throughout the image. Add tinted gesso to areas where there are highlights.

Use opacity to diminish areas of the collage that might overpower the structure and value of your subject.

Continue adding layers of transparent and opaque paint until you achieve your desired results.

A NOTE ABOUT PAINT LAYERING

Think about the qualities of the paint when layering. If you are using transparent paint to achieve stronger color or value, then you'll have to use lots of layers. An opaque paint will yield stronger color and value but will appear flat and will not have the subtlety of the shifting colors of transparent layers. Matte medium will accept paint differently than your original surface accepts paint.

A NEW WEAVE

I know that not every painting is the masterpiece I was hoping it would be. I may put a less-than-favorite piece away for another day or I may find myself looking at it and deciding that I like parts of it but not the whole of it. That's when I take scissors in hand.

MATERIALS LIST
brayer
piece of art
polymer or soft gel
scissors

TECHNIQUE ONE: WEAVE IT
You can do this using several different pieces.

1 Cut one piece of art into horizontal strips.

2 Cut another piece of art into vertical strips.

3 Weave the pieces together.

4 Glue the weaving to your background with polymer or soft gel.

5 Press with a brayer.

A New Weave
Sandra Duran Wilson

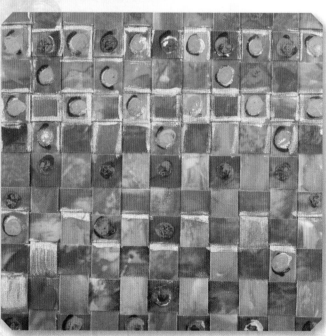

A NEW WEAVE
from *Mixed Media Revolution* by Darlene Olivia McElroy and Sandra Duran Wilson

74

VISIT CREATEMIXEDMEDIA.COM/ADVENTURES-IN-MIXED-MEDIA FOR BONUS CONTENT.

TECHNIQUE TWO: ALL MIXED UP

For this technique you need only one piece of art.

1 Cut the work into strips or sections, vertical or horizontal.

2 Rearrange the strips in a different order than the original or break them up by inserting space between them.

3 Glue them to your background with polymer soft gel.

4 Press with a brayer.

5 Let dry.

MORE IDEAS
- Paint the new piece, leaving some of the underlying paintings showing through.
- Use gold leaf or another embellishment to jazz it up.
- Slightly offset your strips so they are not in perfect alignment.

COFFEE, METAL FLAKES, YARN & STAMPS

In this project you'll use a little of this and a bit of that—elements you may well have around your house or art-making area. I love to drink quality brewed coffee when I wake up in the morning. However, I've learned to keep some inexpensive instant coffee around at all times. Instant coffee crystals mixed with a little water make a rich burnt umber color that looks great on a gessoed panel. Any crystals that don't dissolve all the way add texture. I love how thin metal flakes lend excitement to a simple piece. Vintage postage stamps are some of my favorites for adding those sweet spots that bring the piece together. Yarn supplies fascinating texture and color. In this project I use silk sari yarn. If you have other kinds of silky yarn available, feel free to use that.

MATERIALS LIST

gel medium

instant coffee crystals

light red paint

metal flakes

multi-textured yarn

Neocolor II crayon

paintbrush

paper towel

pre-gessoed panel or canvas

vintage postage stamp

water

white acrylic paint

Beginner's Mind
Coffee, yarn, metal flakes and acrylic on wood panel

COFFEE, METAL FLAKES, YARN AND STAMPS
from *Wabi-Sabi Art Workshop* by Serena Barton

VISIT CREATEMIXEDMEDIA.COM/ADVENTURES-IN-MIXED-MEDIA FOR BONUS CONTENT.

1

Start with a pre-gessoed panel or canvas board. Dip a damp paintbrush into instant coffee crystals. Brush a clump of coffee onto the panel.

2

Brush gel medium thickly onto the coffee area. Tilt the board up and toward you so a little of the coffee drips down to the bottom of the panel.

3

Use your brush to smear a bit of the coffee outward.

4

Sprinkle a small amount of metal flakes into the area of the piece covered with gel medium.

5

Collage a vintage postage stamp in the upper-right corner of the panel. Brush white paint over the stamp and blot the excess, partially obscuring the stamp.

6

Collage two strands of multi-textured yarn, placing one strand on each side of the coffee area.

7

Brush a small amount of light red paint under the yarn line to the right of the coffee area.

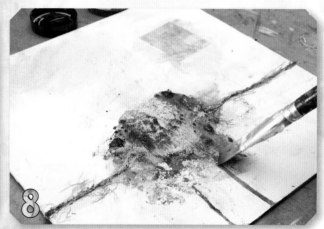

8

Brush a little of the red paint near the bottom of the coffee area.

⑨

Use a Neocolor II crayon to lightly sketch in text in the upper part of the piece. Use a paper towel to rub in and take up most of the text, leaving only a hint of it.

Portal

Plaster, PanPastels, coffee, tea and vintage button on wood panel

I added instant coffee and grains of tea to this plaster piece to give it a natural aged effect.

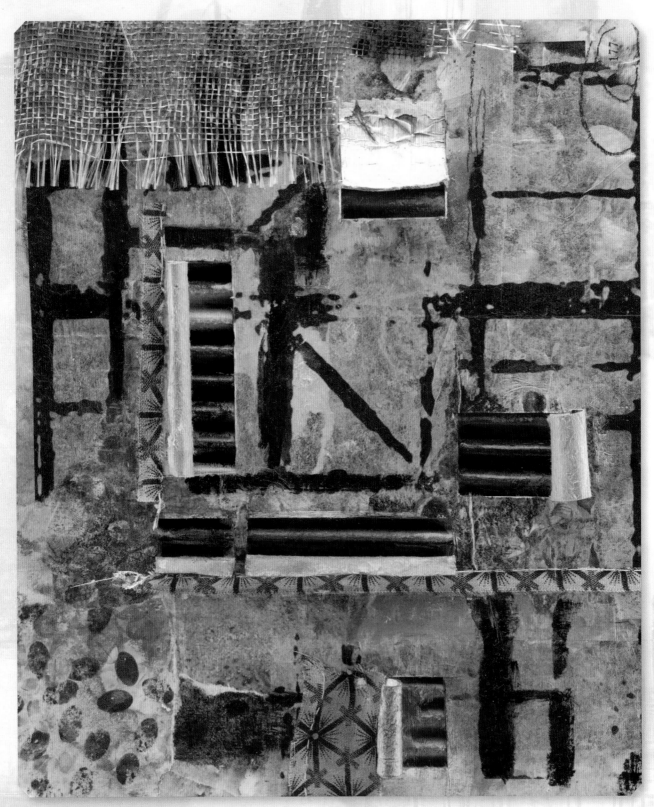

CARDBOARD COLLAGE
from *Flavor for Mixed Media* by Mary Beth Shaw

CARDBOARD COLLAGE

My name is Mary Beth Shaw, and I am a pack rat. I save all sorts of things because I can see potential in nearly every scrap or recycled item I touch. I swear it is a curse to be like this. Over the years, I have accumulated countless bins of things that I just know I will want to use one day. Take my discarded painted paper towels: I started saving these years ago and have an enormous collection. They can be sewn together to create funky wrapping paper; they can be used in collage; they make pretty packing supplies . . .

This Cardboard Collage was inspired by Katie Kendrick. She does amazing things to cardboard, transforming it in such stunning ways that I can't even figure out how she achieves such beauty. So let's play a little bit and see what we can make.

MATERIALS LIST

- acrylic paints
- collage elements
- craft knife
- fabric
- gel medium
- paintbrush
- pencil
- sanding block
- scrap corrugated cardboard
- screening materials
- stencil

Start with a scrap of ordinary cardboard. Collage assorted elements onto the surface of the board using gel medium. Use a sanding block to remove excess paper from the edges.

Paint out certain geometric areas using a stencil. I am using the same stencil that has been printed on the tissue. The use of similar patterns will make the work cohesive.

Use a craft knife to gently cut away the top layer of paper on the cardboard and then roll the paper back to reveal the corrugation underneath.

Fabric can be glued to areas of the board or the inside of the peeled-back flaps. You could also insert a little message here.

ART REPURPOSED

Think of different ways you can repurpose supplies, scraps or other products you have on hand. For instance, I scanned my hand-cut stencil and then made the inverse image, which I printed on light brown tissue paper. The screen used in this project came off a screen door we replaced in our house. I find that its distressed condition is perfect for my use. And the cardboard itself is used packaging material.

Scrape away the fuzzy paper parts along each cardboard ridge and then paint shadows along the sides.

To complete the project, glue down the screening material using gel medium, the go back for touch-up detail with a pencil.

WHAT'S IN YOUR PANTRY?

Use any size of scrap corrugated cardboard to create little cardboard windows such as the ones in this project. Keep them on hand for use in future pieces so you can easily grab one when you need it. You can paint them, distress them with ink or sandpaper or simply leave them plain. I enjoy putting a word in these windows. When I am sorting through vintage papers, such as old book pages, I paint over all except my favorite words, using white paint. The contrast of the paint with the yellowed paper makes my chosen words really pop out. I glue them onto the cardboard windows in such a way that the flaps fold back to reveal the cryptic words.

FINDING THE SACRED IN THE ORDINARY

In learning to look closely at the moments of our everyday lives, we find abundant inspiration—inspiration that sparks our creative ideas and expression. When we find the sacred in the ordinary—a coincidence, a heart-shaped stone or even a sunrise—we allow for a richer saturation of joy and creativity in our lives. Everyday moments become clearer with meaning—moments that we may have never noticed before. And our creative lives are transformed by the inspiration that comes from simply paying closer attention to the abundance that already exists in the ordinary moments of our lives.

Seeking the sacred in the ordinary not only means finding the importance in seemingly unimportant moments within our everyday lives, but it also means acknowledging the value of treasures that are often long forgotten, unused or left behind. My older sister (who happens to be the featured contributing artist in this section) does an amazing job of this. Perusing the aisles of junk stores, she finds treasures that may seem forlorn and ragged to some, but she sees their beauty, their sacred meaning. A stack of old weathered books, cracked mirrors, ripped and torn letters—she finds them beautiful in their own special way. And often they become lovely and engaging centerpieces for her assemblages, where the ordinary becomes extraordinary.

In this section, we'll set off on a journey to find the sacred, simple beauty in the things we once thought were unimportant. So get out your journals, your cameras, your creative spirit, and let's adventure to a place where everything matters and seemingly insignificant tokens and moments suddenly inspire our creativity with their significance.

Time Flies
Assemblage

Wanting to express the beauty of time and the longings we sometimes have as it passes, I transformed a broken, long-forgotten clock into a meaningful piece of art.

FINDING THE SACRED IN THE ORDINARY
from *Taking Flight* by Kelly Rae Roberts

VISIT CREATEMIXEDMEDIA.COM/ADVENTURES-IN-MIXED-MEDIA FOR BONUS CONTENT.

SEEKING SIMPLE BEAUTY

For years, I wondered why my older sister named her creative business SacredCake. I would densely ask, "SacredCake? I don't get it." It took some years of stumbling through my twenties to emerge on the other side with a view and an understanding that there is indeed simple beauty in everything. Everything, including seemingly ordinary things like the falling of leaves, the sweetness of words, the glorious changing of seasons, and yes, even cake. Brilliant. It has likely been one of my biggest lessons learned in life—and it came from my older sister, whose work and wisdom you will see displayed in this section. She not only appreciates all the details of everyday life, things you and I might pass over as "forgettable," but she also finds the sacred in everyday materials that might otherwise go unnoticed or be thrown away. She takes these very items and turns them into glorious, meaningful art.

So, what exactly does finding the sacred in the ordinary have to do with a creative life? Everything. Everything. Everything. Finding the sacred in the everyday details not only expands our personal gratitude for every ounce of the world's offerings, but it fuels our creative expression. Once we learn to seek simple beauty, we find ourselves surrounded by inspiration that, when collected inside moments of seemingly insignificant details, expands our creative voice. We see things where we didn't see them before. We pay attention. We get inspired. Suddenly, the sky isn't just the sky. Instead, it's full of shades and shapes we didn't stop to pause and notice before— beauty that may inspire a new project idea. Even raindrops, as my friend Nina has taught me, aren't just raindrops. Instead, they are bubbles of rainwater that, if looked closely upon, reveal a mirror image of their surroundings—how beautiful! Just like the raindrops, inside the casing of our everyday lives are small sacred wonders waiting to be noticed and waiting to

spark our creativity. Just as Rauol Vaneigem reminds us, "There are more truths in twenty-four hours of a man's life than in all the philosophies."

DOCUMENTING THE JOURNEY

For me, one of the ways I find beauty and truth in the ordinary is by taking photos of my everyday happenings, of my small discoveries along the way. Some days, I snap photo after photo of treasures I find on my daily walks—the way the sun is setting (reminding me of the birth of possibility and inspiring me to use more yellows and pinks in my paintings), old doorways (signifying so much in their distressed beauty), my feet and shoes (representing literal steps in the journey of life). I also capture images of heart shapes, found in leaves and rocks and wood grain—to me, they represent small but significant speckles of universal loveliness and meaning. All of this photo-taking inspires me to think about how I express my creativity to the world—the colors I am drawn to, the aesthetic I want to capture. It's all right there in my daily life. I just have to pay attention and ordinary things suddenly become anything but.

How about you? Perhaps you're a photographer, already in tune with capturing the small wonders of every day. Is there something you may be missing in the details? Or perhaps you're a mother whose camera has been stashed away, like the china, only coming out for special occasions. What about the special occasion that is today? Perhaps this week you could challenge yourself to carry your camera everywhere. Take a photo of anything and everything that calls to you—your child's colorful stockings, your favorite pair of shoes, the way the light falls onto your skin, the flower that bloomed in your garden today. Pay attention to colors, texture and form, and keep them tucked inside your creative, mindful toolbox.

You will be transformed by how much you see and discover. The idea is that these little discoveries will expand your creative vision, perhaps get you thinking of new ideas, new projects, new color combinations and texture. By the way, this is a great opportunity to start that blog or your journal or a "sacred things" scrapbook as a way to document your findings. It will help you remember to keep looking, paying attention and celebrating the beauty of the details. Your creative spirit will thank you!

Now that you're capturing your sacred moments in photographs and writing, go a step further and start actually collecting physical mementos of your every-day journeys to use in creative projects. Next time you're on a walk on the beach or in the park, or even while you're window shopping, look for small tokens that call to you. Perhaps it's a crisp autumn-colored leaf or an abandoned piece of weathered wood. Maybe it's your own heart-shaped rock found at the ocean or a handful of seaglass. Think about ways you can use these items in your creative expressions. Could you include your heart-shaped rock in your next piece of jewelry? Perhaps in a sculpture? Could you preserve those few leaves and include them in your next collage? What are some ways you can begin to infuse your sacred-in-the-ordinary items into your work?

In the piece shown here, I used an old, tattered and worn book for my painting. When I found it, I was called to the beauty of its age, its rough edges and the long-forgotten words covering its deserted pages. I thought it would make a lovely and meaningful frame around a painting. This simple, seemingly common and nondescript book now has a new life—it has transcended from ordinary to meaningful. The idea is the same with the *Time Flies* assemblage. Wanting to express the beauty of time and the longings we sometimes have as it passes, I transformed a broken, long forgotten clock into a meaningful piece of art. The wings, fully inspired by my sister, give it a deeper sense of expressiveness—something that was ordinary before now has a new spirit, a new significance.

Is there anything that you could breathe more life into through a creative project? What about that stack of vintage postcards, or that collection of old buttons, or even your daily photographs depicting everyday

treasures? Could they have new life inside a lovely assemblage? Whether you actually use your findings in your creative projects or not, your creative spirit will thank you for beginning to pay attention to the details that hold meaning, to the simple abundance that exists in your everyday life. It's about finding simple significance where perhaps you overlooked it before. It could be the way a stranger opened a door for you as you entered a busy downtown building. Perhaps it's an understanding glance from friend. Or maybe it's a song lyric that grabs a piece of your soul. Whatever it is, try and capture it—in a journal, in a photograph, on your blog. Your creative spirit will begin to notice these things, too, and your inspiration will soar.

Vintage Book Girl
Small mixed-media painting on watercolor paper framed inside a lovely vintage book. You'll learn how to make your own vintage book frame later in this demonstration.

TAKING FLIGHT WITH CONTRIBUTING
ARTIST JENNIFER VALENTINE

KRR: Jennifer, you have taught me so much about thinking twice about my everyday surroundings. Can you tell me how finding the sacred in the ordinary has inspired your creativity?

JV: My creativity is inspired by everyday objects that most people overlook or regard as useless items. In looking closer at things, I experience them in a way that one would witness a life. For instance, when I use a mirror in my work, I think of the life it has had, the faces it has seen, the places it has been, and when it was finally rendered useless . . . and then, somehow, it finds me. I rescue these discarded lives, and each object tells me its own special story. In my work, I marry the various objects together to tell a unique and meaningful tale. Sacredness comes when I can look deeper into the meaning of objects and turn it into an experience.

KRR: I appreciate your being so mindful with your art-making—it becomes about a meaningful experience, not just for you, but for those who are called to it. Tell us about your signature wings, like the ones in *Sacred*. They grace many of your pieces. What is the significance for you?

JV: The significance of the wings is a symbol of escape, freedom and divinity. For this piece, the wings symbolize the freedom and clarity that comes when we realize that, with all of our imperfections, each of us is a sacred being.

KRR: Tell us about what this lovely mirror piece means to you. Does the mirror reflect an inner knowing, a reflection of some kind?

JV: Imperfection inspires me to create. The mirror piece is very meaningful to me. A positive self-image can be abolished by our own negative inner voices. The constant glare of the media says we have to look a certain way in order to achieve acceptance and beauty. This mirror piece communicates the message that we are sacred and beautiful souls, imperfections and all. It reminds me of my own divinity and sacred self.

KRR: What is your advice for those who desire to seek more of the sacred inside a seemingly ordinary life?

JV: Seeking the sacred in the ordinary is mindfulness that can be practiced moment by moment. When you open yourself to all of the goodness that life has to offer, even the simplest activity can become a sacred event. In the perceived ordinariness of our lives, there lies potential. Even if we feel depleted and unable to find joy, the simple idea that we are given this day may be enough to begin the process of finding divinity in our lives.

KRR: Can you give me a recent example of an everyday moment in your life that held more meaning once you looked more closely?

JV: Just the other day I was examining a beautiful autumn leaf and I experienced such childlike wonderment. Suddenly, I found the universe there. How can something so simple yet so complex be an accident?

Sacred

Assemblage by my talented sister and contributing artist, Jennifer Valentine. In this piece, Jennifer communicates the message that we are sacred and beautiful souls, imperfections and all.

LEARNING TO SOAR

I've long admired Jennifer's winged creations, so it was such a joy for me to learn exactly how she makes them when I added them to this vintage book photo frame project. My mind went haywire with creative ideas. I could add these simple-to-make but deliciously distressed wings to just about anything: paintings, assemblages, vintage picture frames, boxes and on and on.

First, I'll show you how to turn a vintage book into a lovely photo frame, transforming an everyday item into an extraordinary centerpiece for a craft project. Then, you'll learn Jennifer's technique for making a set of those gorgeous and delicate wings out of tissue paper and wire. Adding them to your book will create a whimsical and meaningful work of art. So come along with me as we find our creative wings (literally!) and transform something ordinary into something more.

MATERIALS LIST

Materials for Creating a Vintage Book Photo Frame

- 3 bulldog clips
- 3 buttons or other embellishments
- decorative chipboard letters
- fine-grit sandpaper (optional)
- foam brush
- gel medium
- glue stick
- old hardcover book
- pencil
- photograph
- sharp razor blade
- straightedge

Materials for Creating Wings

- about 40" (102cm) 22-gauge wire
- foam brush
- hammer
- heat gun (optional)
- heavy-duty gel medium
- setting mat
- sparkle glaze, or gel medium and loose glitter
- Walnut Stain Distress Ink (Ranger)
- white tissue paper

VISIT CREATEMIXEDMEDIA.COM/ADVENTURES-IN-MIXED-MEDIA FOR BONUS CONTENT.

CREATING A VINTAGE BOOK PHOTO FRAME

When I was younger, my mom taught me how to make photo frames out of vintage books. I've been making them ever since, adding my own touch and embellishments. I'm thrilled to share a bit of my family's creativity with you in this project inspired by both my mom and my sister. All you need is a simple book and a favorite photo.

Position a photograph where you would like it to appear through the front cover of the book. Use a pencil to trace the outline of the photograph onto the cover. If the area you want to frame extends toward the edges of the photo, you'll want to trace an area at least ¼" (6mm) around the edges of the photo instead of tracing the photo itself, as some of the image will be covered later.

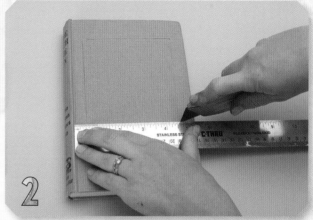

Take a sharp razor blade and, using a straightedge, cut along the pencil lines, pressing hard enough to cut completely through the cover. You may need to score over the same line multiple times with the razor before it cuts completely through the hard cover. Erase the pencil lines if they are still visible.

Using your pencil and straightedge, draw lines to form a smaller square inside the area you just cut out from the cover. Here I drew a square about ½" (1cm) smaller than the first one, but yours can be any size you like.

Open the flap and line up your straightedge with the first line of the inner square. Use your razor to begin cutting through the interior pages of the book. You can apply a lot of pressure and score the line several times for a deeper shadow-box effect, or apply lighter pressure to create a shallower frame. Remove the cut-out centers of the pages. You may have to play with this a bit to get it even, cutting more as necessary.

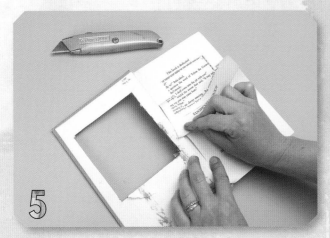

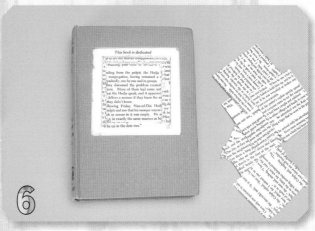

5

Once you have the inner square cut out, page through the first few pages and see if there is any writing you'd like to expose as your top layer. Here, I found the words "This book is dedicated" just above my cut-out square a few pages into the book, so I ripped the first few pages out of the book until this page was the top layer.

6

Use a straightedge and a pencil to draw another square inside the first—this will serve as yet another layer of your frame. Mine is about ¼" (6mm) inside my first cut square. Repeat the process of scoring the lines with your razor and straightedge and removing the inner portion of the pages, cutting as deep or as shallow as you like.

7

Position the photo inside the frame so that the portion of the photo that you want to frame peeks through the inner square. Use your glue stick to adhere it in place.

8

Use a glue stick to adhere some decorative chipboard letters, vintage buttons or other embellishments to the cover beneath or around the photo frame.

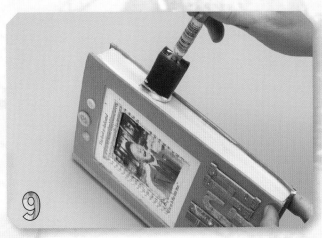

9

Using a foam brush, apply a heavy coat of gel medium to the edges of the pages to seal the book closed (don't worry if you're messy—it will dry clear). Clip a bulldog clip to each edge of the book to hold it tightly together as it dries. Put any finishing touches on your piece that you'd like. Here, I peeled back a bit of the cover around the window that's been cut to create a more distressed look.

CREATING WINGS (CONTRIBUTING ARTIST'S TECHNIQUE BY JENNIFER VALENTINE)

Now for one of my favorite contributor techniques! We're going to put our book photo frame aside while we try Jennifer's unique way of making a lovely set of wings out of wire and tissue paper. Remember, the possibilities are endless. You could make these as small or as large as you'd like, and add them to just about anything—think of your favorite old clock or a decorative vintage bottle. Have fun with it!

STRETCH YOUR WINGS

Use a fine-grit sandpaper to fray the edges of your book if you want to enhance its distressed, vintage look.

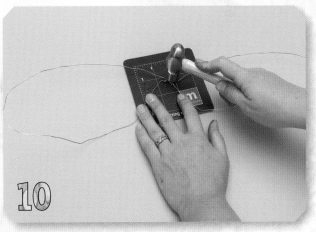

10

Fold the ends of the wire inward until they meet. Twist the ends together in the center to hold them in place, forming a sort of figure eight. Protect your work surface with a setting mat, and use a hammer to pound the center twist flat.

STRETCH YOUR WINGS

Use any kind of tissue paper you want for your wings. Old sewing-pattern tissue paper is one of my favorites for creating a unique, vintage look.

11

Use your hands to shape the two circles of the wire figure eight into the shape of wings, making them as symmetrical as possible.

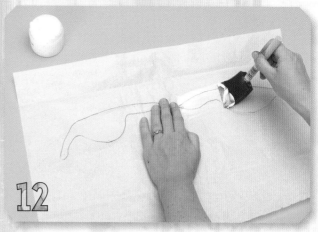

12

Lay the wings on a piece of white tissue paper cut to be slightly more than twice their width. Use a foam brush to totally encase the wings and the surrounding paper in gel medium. It's OK if the tissue paper gets wrinkly, but be careful not to tear it—it can be fragile once moistened by the medium.

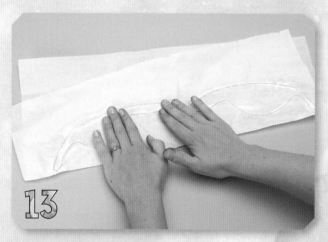

13

Fold over the tissue paper and press it firmly into the gel medium, sandwiching the wire wings. Let it dry completely. (You can speed this process up a bit by using the heat gun if desired.)

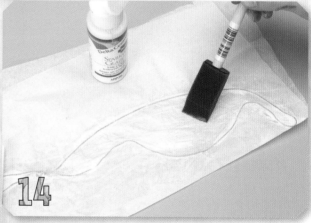

14

Brush a sparkle glaze over the surface of the wings with a foam brush (or brush gel medium onto the surface and then sprinkle it with glitter). Let it dry completely.

VISIT CREATEMIXEDMEDIA.COM/ADVENTURES-IN-MIXED-MEDIA FOR BONUS CONTENT.

15

Rub the Walnut Stain Distress Ink pad gingerly over the surface of the tissue paper to give it a more antique look and to emphasize the lines of the wire. At this point, it's very important that you let the wings dry completely before moving on to the next step.

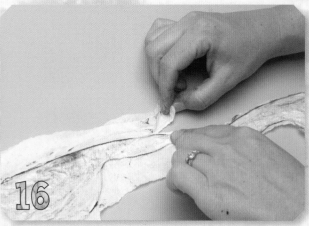

16

Very carefully tear the excess paper away from the edges of the wire to expose the shape of the frame. Be sure to leave the wire encased in the tissue, tearing the tissue only outside of the wire form.

17

Use a dab of heavy-duty gel medium to secure the wings in between some of the pages in the bottom right corner of the photo square. Or you can attach the wings to another project of your choice.

STRETCH YOUR WINGS

If your wings are too translucent, you can add a second layer of tissue paper with gel medium.

I have been married for ten years. Those years have been both long and short depending on the circumstances. For our tenth anniversary, my husband and I decided to do an impromptu wedding vow renewal with friends and family. I wanted to make a small book to commemorate this ceremony. It is also a place to hold some of the memories we've made through the years. So much has happened, both good and bad. However, the most important thing has remained: There is still an us.

10
from *The Elemental Journal* by Tammy Kushnir

MATERIALS LIST

22-gauge copper wire

acrylic paint

awl

craft glue

foam brush

hammer

images printed on photo paper

love notes

nails

natural findings

personal photos

pieces from a wooden box, approximately 2½" × 3" (7cm × 8cm)

plastic test tubes or vials

scissors

string from curtains

strips of bark, approximately 1½" × 7½" (4cm × 19cm)

twigs

wood glue

wooden button with one hole

wooden tag

CAST ASIDE

I went "shopping" in my backyard with my son's help and found the bark used in this journal. You can find these abandoned strips in your backyard and local parks. If you choose to create a book this way, make sure you pick bark that's thick so it can withstand wear and tear.

To assemble the cover, use an awl to punch holes into seven strips of bark measuring approximately 1½" × 7½" (4cm × 19cm). Punch two holes at the top, middle and bottom of each strip, except for the last strips on each side of the cover, which only need one hole at the top, middle and bottom. Connect the strips by threading copper wire in and out of each hole.

Find the spine of the cover by locating the center piece of bark. Punch four holes in the spine in a vertical line: two above the center wire holes and two below.

Disassemble a small wooden box. Paint two pieces of the box with acrylic paint and a foam brush. Hammer two small nails into the side of each piece. These nails will be used to attach the pages to the bark cover.

Attach love notes or personal photos printed onto photo paper to each wooden page with craft glue.

5 Adhere natural findings, such as pebbles or twigs, to the pages with wood glue. I wrote the number 10 on a heart-shaped pebble and glued it to the corner of one page.

6 Thread a 30 " (76cm) piece of curtain string through the two closest center holes from step 2, pulling both ends through so they are inside the cover.

7 Bind the pages together, wrapping the 30 " (76cm) piece of string around the nails. Wrap one end of the string around the top nail of a page a few times and then make a double knot. Wrap the other end of the string around the bottom nail and make a double knot. Move to the second page and repeat, using the same string. As you wrap, pull the string taut so the pages are snug against the cover.

Thread a 20" (51cm) piece of string through the two center holes in the spine, pulling both ends through so they are inside the cover. Wrap the ends of this string around the nails in the second page as you did before.

8 Thread all string ends through the remaining holes in the spine, bringing them outside the cover. Knot the strings together against the spine to secure them.

VISIT CREATEMIXEDMEDIA.COM/ADVENTURES-IN-MIXED-MEDIA FOR BONUS CONTENT.

9 Fill two plastic vials with messages, love notes or bits of nature and slip them beneath the wires inside the front and back covers.

10 Slip twigs beneath the wires in the front cover. Write a message or the word *love* on a wooden tag and secure it with wire or string to the front cover.

INSPIRING HINT

Choose a base that speaks to you. I chose bark for this journal because it appeared to be fragile but was much stronger than it looked. It reminded me of how a marriage can go through troubled times, but when a couple works together, strength is always there.

11 Wrap a 12" (31cm) piece of curtain string around the outside of the journal. Thread both ends through the hole in a wooden button and tighten the string to keep the journal closed.

CHILD WITHIN
from *The Elemental Journal* by Tammy Kushnir

CHILD WITHIN

Hidden within all of us are the hopes and dreams we often forget or repress as we leave our childhoods and enter "reality." If we look through the pain, problems and abandoned ideas we once had, we can find what we loved and embrace it, follow it and thrive in it. This journal is the link between childhood moments and the present digital age of recording it all.

CAST ASIDE

The case used in this journal is the standard packaging for an iPod touch. If you can't track one down, try finding a trading card case used for collecting and storing baseball cards.

MATERIALS LIST

24" × 34" (61cm × 87₂cm) acrylic sheet, ½" (13mm) thick

acrylic cutting knife

Adobe Photoshop

collage images

copy paper

craft glue

cutting mat

foam brush

hard plastic case

ink-jet printer

personal images

scissors

straightedge

transparency paper

white acrylic paint

1 With white acrylic paint and a foam brush, generously paint the inside of a hard plastic case. Print an image of vintage lined paper with the word *journal* in the corner onto transparency paper. Once the paint has dried, glue the image to the inside of the front of the case.

2 Print a picture of a waterfall onto a piece of copy paper and glue it inside the back of the case. Once the glue has dried, paint around the edges of the image.

3 Lay a sheet of acrylic on a cutting mat. Using an acrylic cutting knife and a straightedge, score a rectangle in the acrylic that will fit snugly within the hard plastic case. Snap the acrylic along the scored lines to make a rectangular acrylic card. Repeat this step to make three more cards.

4 Create an image using Adobe Photoshop, combining personal photos and collage images. Add an appropriate journaling phrase to the page. Print the completed image onto transparency paper. Once the ink has dried (some inks take 24–48 hours), glue the right side to the back of an acrylic card so the image shows through but cannot be smudged by fingerprints.

5 Paint the edges and back of the card with white acrylic paint. When painting the back of the card, leave some spaces unpainted for the image on the next card to peek through.

6 Repeat steps 3–4 for the remaining acrylic cards. Once the cards are dry, stack them face up and place them in the painted plastic case.

4

SHARE MIXED MEDIA WITH THE WORLD!

It feels good, doesn't it? Making mixed-media art on par with the very art and artists who first inspired you. Now it's your turn to share your art, your talent, your passion with the world. Whether it's creating winged messengers from Jenny Doh's *Art Saves* or collaborating on a word-based project, as Liz Lamoreux demonstrates, it's your turn. Your turn to inspire others to create mixed media.

The final chapter of this book is not the final chapter of your adventure. It's the first chapter of helping someone else start their own adventure with mixed-media art. Told you it feels good!

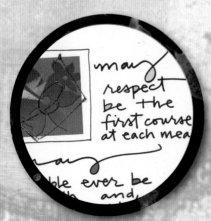

SUSANNA GORDON: WINGED MESSENGER

Art speaks in many ways. It can be used to tell stories, express emotions, and give a voice to those without one. Susanna Gordon's art is about delivering messages to people who need them, messages of hope that inspire thought and promote positivity. Her instantly recognizable "winged messengers" have traveled to Kenya, France, Denmark and even the Great Wall of China. They've made people smile, they've made people ponder, they've brought together a group of artists from around the globe . . . and it all started with a piece of art and an idea.

WINGED MESSENGER: SUSANNA GORDON
from *Art Saves* by Jenny Doh

INSPIRED LESSONS

Get Distracted.
Instead of letting yourself fixate on the parts of your life that cause you stress, give your mind room to wander. Susanna's favorite way to escape is to grab her camera and head out for a walk in a local park. She allows herself to soak in her surroundings and quickly finds herself too distracted by the beauty around her to focus on whatever had been worrying her.

Take Advice.
Being on the outside looking in can provide unique insight, so if someone you trust offers you advice, consider taking it. Susanna's decision to pursue higher education in the arts was influenced by an admired teacher, who urged her to submit a portfolio to a nearby art and design college. The recommendation was spot-on. Susanna wound up attending that school, where she discovered a passion for photography.

VISIT CREATEMIXEDMEDIA.COM/ADVENTURES-IN-MIXED-MEDIA FOR BONUS CONTENT.

Make It Happen.

Everyone has something to contribute to the greater good, and it's up to you to get out there and do it. Once Susanna had developed the idea for her winged messenger project, she didn't wait to get it off the ground . . . she jumped right in and began leaving her inspirational art pieces around her own neighborhood before branching out to the far corners of the world.

PAY IT FORWARD

Few things in the world are more powerful than a positive push. A smile. A word of optimism and hope. A "you can do it" when things are tough.
—Richard M. DeVos

SPREADING HER WINGS

The idea of winged envelopes flying through the grass was based on an illustration Susanna drew for her husband when they were living apart, in two separate countries. She then saw a blog post by Madelyn Mulvaney and became inspired to write encouraging messages onto the envelopes. "I thought they would look beautiful moving through tall grass in a field," says Susanna. She posted the image on her blog, and began receiving requests from fellow artists who wanted to place the thought-provoking art pieces around their own communities. Susanna poured herself into crafting a new set of one-of-a-kind envelopes, each featuring a handwritten message of positivity. In return, she asked that each participant send her a story chronicling the placement of the messengers or photographs of the pieces in their new environments. And with that, the winged messenger project was born.

Now Susanna creates her winged messengers in her art room—emblazoned with inspirational messages like "your opinion matters" and "you're a work of art"—to send to participants spanning the globe. "If I go a period of time without creating, it feels as though I am missing something deep in my being," she says. "I get antsy, like I'm not doing what I should be doing, what I want to be doing. There's a sense of fulfillment when I work on my artwork, whether the piece is turning out the way I want it to or not, simply because I am creating."

WHEN THE GOING GETS TOUGH

Says Susanna Gordon: "When the going gets tough, the tough allows herself a moment of angst and self-pity, then makes a plan and moves on."

IN SUSANNA'S OWN WORDS: GIVE IT AWAY

"I love the notion of art that's made to give away to others. It benefits the artist as well as the recipient, and it encourages creativity. My challenge for you is to make one piece of artwork today—it can be something as simple as a sketch on a piece of paper or as elaborate as a finished painting, as long as it's a work you've crafted by hand—and then give it to someone without asking for anything in return."

VISIT CREATEMIXEDMEDIA.COM/ADVENTURES-IN-MIXED-MEDIA FOR BONUS CONTENT.

IN SUSANNA'S OWN WORDS: COLLABORATE

"Combine your efforts with the efforts of other like-minded people, and you'll be able to achieve things that are greater than what any one person could accomplish alone. The power of collaboration is what has truly allowed my winged messengers to take flight. What started as my own simple, little art project turned into something much bigger, and much better, with the help of strangers around the world."

IN SUSANNA'S OWN WORDS: FREE ART

"There is something liberating about creating a piece of artwork and leaving it for a stranger to find to keep for free. For me, it's a way of returning something creative back into the world that inspires me. I like to imagine that the messages on my pieces will also resonate with whoever finds it and decides to keep it, or perhaps that person will pass it on to someone in his or her life."

USE YOUR KNOWLEDGE

Susanna says, "Actively use your technical skills—even those that aren't art-related—to make an impact. At the end of the literacy program I volunteered with, a local book publisher bound each student's images and story into a hardcover book free of charge. I was so moved by this act of generosity, and I know that those children will treasure those one-of-a-kind books for many years."

EXPRESSING HERSELF

The process of creating—letting your mind wander and exploring the possibilities that exist in life—allows you to tap into parts of yourself that are unreachable otherwise. Says Susanna: "Art has always been a way to express how I'm feeling and what I'm thinking about at that moment of my life. I want to visually express those ideas to others, but most often art-making has been a way for me to figure out how I feel about something." Coping with painful emotions like grief and anger is never easy, but when you give yourself room to openly express what you're going through in your art, you take an active approach to dealing with your feelings.

The death of Susanna's father when she was only twenty-one left her devastated. She wanted to grieve the loss of the man who played such an important part in her life, but she found herself unable—until she discovered a way to commemorate him through her art. Along with a fellow blogger, Stephanie Hilvitz, she cohosted an online Dia de los Muertos-themed event called "Dia de Bloglandia," which invited participants to celebrate their loved ones by posting stories and photographs of handmade altars designed to honor the deceased. Says Susanna: "The most powerful part was the stories that were told about the dead; some of them were funny; some of them were sad; all of them were full of love."

A THOUSAND WORDS

Visual media like photography and painting bring storytelling to its most basic form and make sharing personal narratives accessible to everyone. Volunteering at a literacy program for children created by two special teachers at the school, was an opportunity for Susanna to harness the power of art as a universal language and to use it to change young lives. The participants in her class ranged in age from six to eight years old, and all had struggled with traditional techniques for learning to read. But when art became part of the equation, the students found a new way to express themselves.

Using donated cameras, the children first documented their lives through photography—taking snapshots of their family, friends and surroundings—and then crafted stories to accompany the images. It didn't matter if the grammar was correct or if the spelling was perfect. That would come later. What mattered was that the students were reading and writing. Says Susanna: "These students had repeatedly failed their reading and writing assessments, and yet they 'got it.' They understood that art could be a way to visually express what someone was feeling inside or trying to say."

Susanna has taken a simple idea of sharing beauty and with the help of the arts community, turned it into a unique phenomenon. "Each of us can use our creative voice to make a difference in this world," she says. "It's just a matter of doing it."

CONNECT YOUR COMMUNITY

Schools are cutting back on funding for arts programs, independent galleries are closing, non-profit art centers are struggling, and it's all happening in our own communities. Find a local cause that speaks to you and get involved. You'll not only help an organization that's in need, but you'll also fuel creative connections in your neighborhood.

VISIT CREATEMIXEDMEDIA.COM/ADVENTURES-IN-MIXED-MEDIA FOR BONUS CONTENT.

WINGED MESSENGERS

Before one of Susanna's charming winged envelopes can inspire someone else, she has to settle into her studio, roll up her sleeves, and make it. Beginning with a blank piece of paper, she layers paint, pastels and messages of positivity to create each one-of-a-kind winged messenger before sending it off to one of her eager participants. This project will teach you how to craft your own winged messengers using Susanna's original techniques, but it's up to you to decide what words to share and who the lucky recipient of the finished piece will be.

MATERIALS LIST

acrylic paints-black, white and yellow

black pastel

felt

foam brush

glue

ink-jet printer

paintbrushes

scissors

straightedge

thick, uncoated paper or cardstock

1

Create a wing template from the felt, and use it to trace a wing onto thick paper or cardstock. Flip the template over, and use it to trace a second wing. You will need two wings for each envelope—one left-facing wing and one right-facing wing.

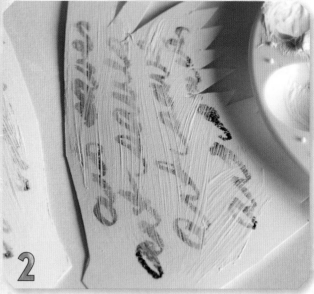

2

Using black pastel, write messages onto each of the wings. Mix together the yellow and white acrylic paints to achieve a pale yellow hue, and then apply a thin coat of paint over the top of each wing. Allow to dry thoroughly.

3

Add feathers and accent lines to the wings using a thin paintbrush and black acrylic paint.

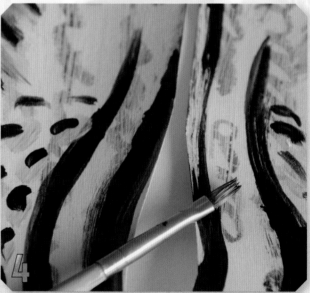

4

Once dry, apply additional accents with white and yellow acrylic paints.

5 Cut a rectangle out of the same paper as the wings to create the envelope. Following the same steps used to embellish the wings, add words to the face of the envelope with black pastel and apply a layer of pale yellow acrylic paint over the top.

6 Using black acrylic paint, add a line to represent the flap on the envelope and a border around the outer edge, as well as the message. Affix the wings onto the back side of the envelope and allow them to dry completely. When finished, the project measures approximately 15" × 8" (38cm × 20cm).

REVEALING THE POET WITHIN

In this section, you will dip your toes into the world of poetry and play with words. You will discover the joys of having a Word Toolbox and learn about how having words available in front of you makes it so much easier to free the poet within you. Even if poetry hasn't always had a place on a shelf in your home, I encourage you to read on (because I just know you will discover the poems that live inside you).

WORDS DISCOVERED: CREATING A WORD TOOLBOX

A favorite book that makes poetry accessible is *Poem-crazy* by Susan Wooldridge. I was lucky enough to take a class from Susan in 2007. After her workshop, I began to realize that a writer can have a "toolbox of words" available to make the writing experience just a little bit easier. This toolbox doesn't refer to the words we carry around in our heads at any given moment. Instead this toolbox can come in the form of lists of words, pages literally torn out of old dictionaries, journals filled with phrases. This toolbox becomes a mine holding just the right word that can lead to just the right phrase to begin a poem.

Task: Gather words and begin to create a Word Toolbox.

Notes: Grab a book off your bookshelf (the first one you see is a good place to start). Open to random pages and write down a word or two from each page. It is a good idea to let your eyes jump from word to word to find the word that stands out to you. Write down at least twenty words. Look at your word list. Is it interesting to you? Do the words jump out? Do they make you think? Do you feel a desire to pick up your pencil and write? If not, I invite you to try this exercise again, perhaps with another book. This time, look for words that are juicy, beautiful, messy, sticky, solid. Look for words that

invite images of action and stillness. Look for words that twirl around on your tongue. Write down the word that scares you, makes you smile and invites you to say, "Yes!" Do not be afraid of the word you do not know; add it to your list. Begin to collect your words in an accessible location. Maybe tape them in your journal, gather them in a document on your computer, or create a special Word Toolbox from an old cigar box or basket. The key is to be able to find them quickly when you want to write.

Think about other places where you might find words:
- Go to a thrift store and buy an old dictionary. When you sit down to write, rip out a page (really, you can do it) to use as your word list.
- Use vocabulary cards (you can buy these at a bookstore or online) and gather a few in a pile as part of your Word Toolbox.
- Visit the library and make word lists from the books you find there.
- When you are finished with a magazine, rip out a few articles, grab a favorite pen and circle the words that stand out to you in the articles.

As you write down your words, I invite you to pause before capturing

REVEALING THE POET WITHIN
from *Inner Excavation* by Liz Lamoreux

VISIT CREATEMIXEDMEDIA.COM/ADVENTURES-IN-MIXED-MEDIA FOR BONUS CONTENT.

an entire phrase verbatim because that phrase really belongs to the author of whatever you are reading.

The first time I remember really thinking about poetry was when I read Carl Sandburg's poem "Fog" in the fourth grade. I recall attempting to visualize fog arriving like cat's feet, but as a northern Indiana girl, I struggled with this image. To me, fog was thick and never-ending and meant being really quiet in the backseat as one of my parents drove at night. Now, living in the Pacific Northwest, I can close my eyes and see fog stepping quickly, lightly, yet solidly across Puget Sound, and I smile with an understanding of Sandburg's choice of words.

Poetry continued to come in and out of my life in positive ways (an eighth-grade girl's attempt to make sense of the world through poetry, a teenager memorizing Langston Hughes' "Theme for English B") until my senior year in high school when it suddenly seemed inaccessible and, well, hard to understand. Poetry, or at least "academic poetry," and I took a break.

Then, in my late twenties I read Derek Walcott's poem "Love After Love" and everything shifted. This poem held up a mirror and seemed to say, "Look closer." I soon found myself in the poetry section of a local bookstore sitting on the floor with Mary Oliver and Sharon Olds and Billy Collins, and again, I heard the whispers, "You are not alone."

Through the encouragement of an online community of others who appreciated, wrote and read poetry, I began writing poems as part of my writing practice. I also started sharing some of them on my blog.

Now this is the part where I am concerned I might lose you. What I have learned is that many people have had experiences like I did in high school where poetry simply becomes inaccessible. We read a poem and feel like we just "don't get it." Then a teacher tells us what the poem is supposed to mean, and we sit there thinking, "Seriously? I do not get poetry."

If this sounds like your experience, please know you are in the right place. In this section, we simply begin with words.

When I explained to Susan Tuttle that I wanted her to gather words to create a poem for this section, she surprised me with the explanation that she already does this. Before she writes, she gathers words from her vintage book collection to use as prompts and inspiration for her writing. "Lodging of the Heart" is Susan's poem inspired by collected words.

Finding words in unexpected places is a great way to not only bring in words you might not use on a regular basis, but also to push yourself to find another way to say a phrase or evoke a feeling. Imagine finding words in a chemistry textbook or your child's favorite book or a cooking magazine. Using a vintage book might reintroduce you to words you haven't heard used since your childhood or teach you words from the childhoods of your grandparents.

LODGING OF THE HEART
SUSAN TUTTLE
cloaked in blessed guard
is the lodging of the heart;
a home of deep and steady joy;
where pain is mere scrawls etched on the walls of
spirit—self-deceiving fear that bows to
imagined superiors.

As she turns her face inward
toward stillness
she glimpses worth and wishes self-denied,
shimmering below the current,
like gold coins carved with enchanted things like
butterflies, garlands and stars;
she recognizes them as her birthright
all hers
waiting to be grasped and
embraced.

ON THE PAGE: JUST WRITE

Your Word Toolbox becomes a source of inspiration and word possibilities for your writing as you seek the poetry within you.

Task: Gather your Word Toolbox and use one of the following prompts as a starting point for writing some "poetic phrases" that are probably going to look and read a lot like a poem:

• I begin . . .
• I am . . .
• I stand . . .
• I see a woman/a man . . .

Notes: Use words from your Word Toolbox to get started or when you get stuck. String those words together and see where they take you. If it feels more comfortable to change "I" to "she" or "he," please do so. You will note Susan's poem is in the third person and retains an intimacy that these prompts invite. Think about similar two- or three-word phrases that begin with I (or she/he) that could be additional prompts for your writing.

WORDS DISCOVERED: GATHER & SHARE

Writing is often thought of as a solitary exercise, but in this section, we explore a few ways to collaborate with others using the written word. Hopefully this section will be a springboard for you to create your own collaborative writing exercises and experiences with the people in your life.

In this next writing exercise, you revisit the "Creating a Word Toolbox" exercise. This time, you will work with a friend and share the words you have discovered as prompts for a collaborative poetry exercise.

Task: Pull out a book from your bookshelf, gather a list of words, and trade that list with a friend who has done the same. Then write a poem inspired by and using some words from this traded list.

Notes: You might use only one word from the list your friend gives you; just experience the thoughts and phrases that were shared.

Example: Contributor Stephanie Lee and I traded word lists and then each wrote a poem inspired by the list. The word lists are included here because you might find a few words you want to use as prompts for your own poem.

VISIT CREATEMIXEDMEDIA.COM/ADVENTURES-IN-MIXED-MEDIA FOR BONUS CONTENT.

The word list I sent Stephanie:

delicate
presence
labor
twig
petal
ample
slope
violet
hum
shimmer
wander
golden
flux
scatter
speckle
farewell
whole
plunge
voyage
grace
heartbeat
sojourn
mystic
blaze
exchange
recover
earthquake
vine
sacrament
vision
ash
sun-flecked
crumb
peony
lavish
narrow
cushion
creak
transparent
extravagance

The word list Stephanie sent me:

vein
leaning/lean
sage
highway
goldbeater
crimson
sprawling/sprawl
moss
corner
church
anxious
write
regret
dialogue
madness
silver
delay
time
wind
bible
entry
swag
crisp
postcard
seven
arch
stone
mist
habit
smoky
Tuesday
edge
true
river
virago
time
fish
Arthur
native
linger

STEPHANIE'S POEM:

A heartbeat at the end of a broken twig
where ash and grace and sun-flecked rain
are kneaded for a compress on the wound
Vision in flux, the sky blankets in wait
Until a fist of petals hums through the splitting salve
Opening.
An ample, earthquake soul takes its first breath

MY POEM:

Unclenching fear, I find
sprawling moss-covered twisting fallen trees
and crimson crooning grosbeaks

Arching my body to look closer, I see
wind twirling pages of regret
and smoky highways littered with habits

Inhaling deeply, I know
crisp, birthing-Spring Tuesdays
and the hope of lingering time

THE RIPPLE EFFECT OF INSPIRATION

"When we focus our energy toward constructing a passionate, meaningful life, we are tossing a pebble into the world, creating a beautiful ripple of inspiration. When one person follows a dream, tries something new, or takes a daring leap, everyone nearby feels that energy and before too long they are making their own daring leaps and inspiring yet another circle."—Christine Mason Miller, from *Ordinary Sparkling Moments*

Imagine a landscape filled with trash and debris; a bleak expanse of lifeless gray. As you scan the horizon, you suddenly notice a burst of color. Amidst a sea of rubbish, there is a thriving garden—flowers and plants, growth and beauty. Over time, you see that garden blossom, aware that the seeds it has created are being quietly scattered in every direction. Before long more flowers take root, new gardens burst forth and your world has slowly transformed. In a culture that has no shortage of bad news and dire predictions, this is the chain of events you create when you pursue your calling on any level. Every step taken toward your most passionate, meaningful life is the highest service you can offer the world—every single step.

A quick glance at some of my most recent inspired moments offers these examples:

• Hearing a close friend talk about his daily practice of spiritual study.

• Perusing a fellow blogger's travel photos.

• Watching my niece and nephews create their own art books on my dining room table.

• Listening to a friend explain that she turned down a job offer because she knew it wasn't right, even though she had no other leads.

These moments did not involve extraordinary feats of daring or risk on the part of any of those I was observing; they came about because each person was sharing his or her own unique ideas, adventures, experiences and creative flairs. Because I happened to be a fortunate witness, I was rewarded with light and inspiration. My friends and family likely weren't aware they were inspiring me. They were just being themselves, and in doing so, shined a lantern on my path.

THE RIPPLE EFFECT OF INSPIRATON
from *Desire to Inspire* by Christine Mason Miller

> IT'S LESS ABOUT PUSHING TOWARD THE EDGE OF SOME GIGANTIC COURAGEOUS RISK AND MORE ABOUT NUDGING GENTLY TOWARD THE TRUTH. EVEN THE SMALLEST STEPS COUNT.
>
> -Anne Carmack

MAKE IT REAL

"Bold generosity is the best response to widespread allegations of scarcity. Inspiration spreads more acts of courageous generosity."—Marianne Elliott

It bears repeating: Every step taken toward your most passionate, meaningful life is the highest service you can offer the world. When you honor the sparkle within you—as a mother, a gardener, a runner—you light the way for others to do the same for themselves. You can set an example for possibility and passion by doing something as simple as taking an art class, writing an authentic blog or preparing a beautiful dinner party. The world needs your spark—your beautifully unique and powerful spirit—and every step, no matter how small, matters.

WHETHER WE CROSS CERTAIN ACCOMPLISHMENTS OFF OUR LIFE LISTS OR SIT IN LOTUS FOR THE NEXT FORTY YEARS, IT ALL MATTERS. WITHOUT PLANNING IT, NAMING IT, THINKING IT, DESIGNING IT, COLORING IT, TEACHING IT—IT ALL MATTERS WITHOUT ANYONE EVER EVEN KNOWING ABOUT IT.

-Pixie Campbell

Photo of Christine Mason Miller by Jen Gray Blackburn

EXERCISES

SMALL STEPS, BIG IMPACT
CREATED BY CHRISTEN OLIVAREZ

"The key to staying focused on this path lies in my daily journal writing. It's on those pages that I remind myself of what I want to give, what I have to offer and what I'm most grateful for."—Christen Olivarez

I have an art journal on my desk that I work on every day, using whatever supplies are available—usually paint, masking tape, pens and maybe a stamp. Some days I'm only able to paint a background; others allow time to record my feelings. At the end of each week, every tiny step I've taken results in a journal page that is dripping with emotion and authenticity.

My office colleagues became fascinated by this process and have since started daily work on their own journals. Little by little, we are each making a difference in our own lives. My daily journal habit was not merely noticed by those around me, it made a big enough impact to inspire them into action.

The following exercise is an adaptation of something I do every day. It shows that spending as little as five minutes a day feeding your creative soul will add up to something more meaningful than expected. Each step will be done on a different day and should take no more than five minutes.

Day One: Supplies
Give yourself five minutes to gather your supplies for the week. You will need an art journal or small canvas, scraps of paper, two to three colors of acrylic paint, gel medium and a paintbrush. I like to do this at my desk at work, where I also have extra pens, tissues and glue.

Day Two: The Foundation
To create a background, squeeze a few drops of different paint colors onto your canvas and use your fingers to spread them out. Be careful not to mix them too much or they will become muddy. Don't be afraid to leave some areas of your canvas white.

Artwork and photos by Christen Olivarez

THE RIPPLE EFFECT OF INSPIRATON
from *Desire to Inspire* by Christine Mason Miller

Day Three: Texture

Apply paint to a pen cap or marker cap and stamp it repeatedly on your background for some texture. Use a tissue to lift up some of the paint and then stamp with other objects—use fingerprints to create a scallop edge and the side of a pencil for stamped lines.

Day Four: Layers

Tear up scraps of paper—receipts, notes, fortunes and wallpaper. Anything will work great! Apply gel medium to the front and back of the scraps and adhere them to your page.

Day Five: More Layers!

Add more paint texture—dab it with a paper towel, wipe some off, smear it. Be willing to experiment.

Day Six: Joy

On the canvas, write a list of small things that bring you great joy.

Day Seven: The Final Touches

Take a good look at your canvas. Is there anything else you'd like to add, cover up or try? Add the final touches, date your journal page and you're finished!

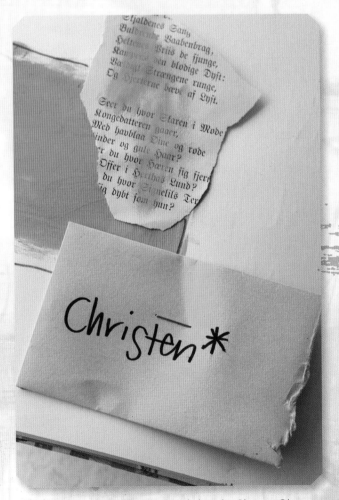

Artwork and photo by Christen Olivarez

WE DON'T KNOW WHERE AND WHEN THE RIPPLES OF INSPIRATION COME ASHORE. BUT THEY DO TRAVEL!

-Andrea Kreuzhage

ONE ACTION AT A TIME
CREATED BY CAROLYN RUBENSTEIN

"If we decide to believe in ourselves, then nothing can diminish our potential."—Carolyn Rubenstein

Have you ever thought, "Why try? I am just one person. What difference can I make?" I imagine many of us have had this thought now and then—even those we look to as heroes and champions. This thought—this inkling of doubt—when recognized, is a magical gift. Are you ready to begin unraveling this gift?

Step One: Recognize Thoughts That Question Your Potential.

Some examples:

"I only have a few dollars to donate, what difference will that make?"

"Why would Alex want to hear from me? I'm sure she has other friends to console her right now."

"I'm not an expert. Why would anyone care what I have to say?"

Step Two: Write Down Those Thoughts—Make Them Tangible.

Thoughts like these typically produce the same result: inaction. We back away and choose to avoid the possibility that maybe we're wrong, that maybe we can help. Consider instead that perhaps the world is waiting for us (for you!) to do something, even if it seems insignificant from your perspective.

Step Three: Challenge the Thoughts Through Action.

After writing down your negative thought, challenge it with an action you can take to prove it wrong (the smaller and easier, the better).

Let's refer to this action as an itty-bitty action. (Much less scary, right?) Some examples:

"I can (and will) donate two dollars to this cause."

"I am going to write Alex a thoughtful note and let her know I am here to support her."

"Someone like me would care—she would want to hear from a 'non-expert.' I'm going to share my thoughts and trust my colleague will be gracious and listen without judgment."

Step Four: Keep a Sacred Change Diary.

Each time you take an action that challenges a limiting thought, record your experience in your Sacred Change Diary. How did it make you feel? How did your friend respond? How did your efforts, insights or contributions make an impact you hadn't expected?

Some examples:

"I donated two dollars to the cause and it made me feel like I was part of a larger community making a difference."

"I mailed a letter to Alex with a bag of my favorite tea. She called the next day and said it was exactly what she needed."

"I spoke with my co-worker about my thoughts on this situation and he has decided to change the focus of our project. This inspired another division to shift their work in the same direction—I had no idea that would happen!"

This journal serves as a reminder that the actions you take will reinforce your potential—threatening (and powerful) evidence for the gremlins that creep up and challenge your ability to make a difference.

After you've experienced the power and impact small actions can make, share this magical gift with others. By sharing this exercise, you will empower others to begin their own inspiring acts and see how far one person's actions can reach along the beautiful ripple that is created. Imagine if you complete twenty-one small actions in as many days and then share this exercise with twenty-one other individuals who follow your example. That's 462 actions and one tremendously inspiring ripple effect!

Wholehearted passion changes the world one person, one action, at a time.

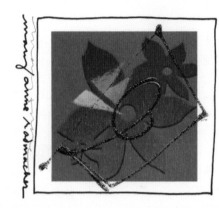

may
respect
be the
first course
at each meal.

may
the table ever be
big enough and,
at the
ring of
the bell,

may
there always be
discovered a
friend at
the door.

Artwork by Mary Anne Radmacher

THE RIPPLE EFFECT OF INSPIRATON
from *Desire to Inspire* by Christine Mason Miller

ABOUT THE CONTRIBUTORS

Art Journal Freedom
by Dina Wakley

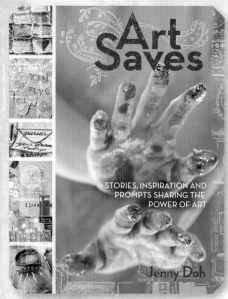

Art Saves
by Jenny Doh

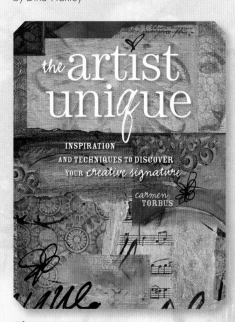

The Artist Unique
by Carmen Torbus

Creative Awakenings
by Sheri Gaynor

Creative Thursday

by Marisa Anne

The Declaration of You!

by Jessica Swift and Michelle Ward

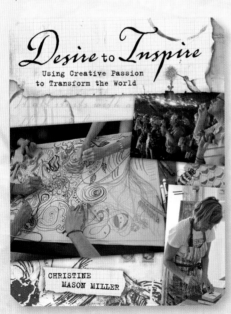

Desire to Inspire

by Christine Mason Miller

The Elemental Journal

by Tammy Kushnir

Flavor for Mixed Media

by Mary Beth Shaw

Inner Excavation

by Liz Lamoreux

Journal Fodder 365

by Eric M. Scott and David R. Modler

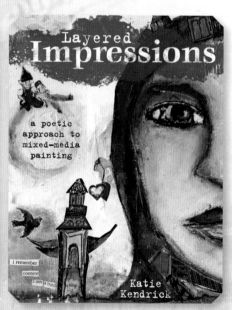

Layered Impressions

by Katie Kendrick

Mixed Media Painting Workshop

by Jean Pederson

Mixed Media Revolution

by Darlene Olivia McElroy and
Sandra Duran Wilson

Stencil Girl

by Mary Beth Shaw

Taking Flight

by Kelly Rae Roberts

Wabi-Sabi Art Workshop

by Serena Barton

125

INDEX

Amy Jones is an associate content developer for North Light Books. She is the co-editor of *Zen Doodle: Tons of Tangles*. You can frequently find her trying mixed-media techniques from the books she edits or reading British literature.

Adventures in Mixed Media Art. Copyright © 2014 by North Light Books. Manufactured in China. All rights reserved. No part of this book may be reproduced in any form or by any electronic or mechanical means including information storage and retrieval systems without permission in writing from the publisher, except by a reviewer who may quote brief passages in a review. Published by North Light Books, an imprint of F+W Media, Inc., 10151 Carver Road, Suite 200, Blue Ash, Ohio, 45242. (800) 289-0963. First Edition.

 Other fine North Light Books are available from your favorite bookstore, art supply store or online supplier. Visit our website at fwmedia.com.

18 17 16 15 14   5 4 3 2 1

DISTRIBUTED IN CANADA BY FRASER DIRECT
100 Armstrong Avenue
Georgetown, ON, Canada L7G 5S4
Tel: (905) 877-4411

DISTRIBUTED IN THE U.K. AND EUROPE
BY F&W MEDIA INTERNATIONAL, LTD
Brunel House, Forde Close, Newton Abbot, TQ12 4PU, UK
Tel: (+44) 1626 323200, Fax: (+44) 1626 323319
Email: enquiries@fwmedia.com

DISTRIBUTED IN AUSTRALIA BY CAPRICORN LINK
P.O. Box 704, S. Windsor NSW, 2756 Australia
Tel: (02) 4560 1600; Fax: (02) 4577 5288
Email: books@capricornlink.com.au

ISBN 13: 978-1-4403-3673-7

Edited by Amy Jones
Designed by Elyse Schwanke
Production coordinated by Jennifer Bass

METRIC CONVERSION CHART

To convert	to	multiply by
Inches	Centimeters	2.54
Centimeters	Inches	0.4
Feet	Centimeters	30.5
Centimeters	Feet	0.03
Yards	Meters	0.9
Meters	Yards	1.1

Ideas. Instruction. Inspiration.

Receive FREE downloadable bonus materials when you sign up for our free newsletter at CreateMixedMedia.com.

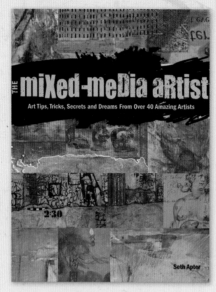

Find the latest issues of *Cloth Paper Scissors* on newsstands, or visit shop.clothpaperscissors.com.

These and other fine North Light products are available at your favorite art and craft retailer, bookstore or online supplier. Visit our websites at createmixedmedia.com and artistsnetwork.tv.

Follow Create Mixed Media for the latest news, free wallpapers, free demos and chances to win FREE BOOKS!

Get your art in print!

Visit **CreateMixedMedia.com** for up-to-date information on *Incite* and other North Light competitions.